MW00527890

LEGACY
in WOOD

Ryan Wahl

LEGACY
in WOOD

The Wahl Family Boat Builders

Harbour Publishing

Copyright © 2008 Ryan David Wahl

1 2 3 4 5 — 12 11 10 09 08

All rights reserved. No part of this publication may be reproduced, stored in a retrieval system or transmitted, in any form or by any means, without prior permission of the publisher or, in the case of photocopying or other reprographic copying, a licence from Access Copyright, www.accesscopyright.ca, 1-800-893-5777, info@accesscopyright.ca.

Harbour Publishing Co. Ltd
P.O. Box 219, Madeira Park, BC, V0N 2H0
www.harbourpublishing.com

Edited by Betty Keller.
Illustrations by Tia McLennan.
Text design and layout by Warren Clark.
Dust jacket design by Anna Comfort.
Front dust jacket, *The Pagan Isle*, courtesy of Vancouver Maritime Museum.
Back dust jacket, Ed Wahl and family, courtesy of Roald and Violet Wahl.
Front dust jacket flap, gillnet launch sequence, courtesy of Roald and Violet Wahl.

Printed in Canada

Harbour Publishing acknowledges financial support from the Government of Canada through the Book Publishing Industry Development Program and the Canada Council for the Arts, and from the Province of British Columbia through the BC Arts Council and the Book Publishing Tax Credit.

 Canada Council for the Arts **Conseil des Arts du Canada** BRITISH COLUMBIA ARTS COUNCIL
Supported by the Province of British Columbia

Library and Archives Canada Cataloguing in Publication

Wahl, Ryan, 1972-
    Legacy in wood : the Wahl family boat builders / by Ryan Wahl.

    Includes index.
    ISBN 978-1-55017-433-5

    1. Wahl, Ed. 2. Wahl family. 3. Wahl Boatyard—History. 4. Boatbuilders—British Columbia—Biography. 5. Boatbuilding—British Columbia—History. 6. Fishing boats—British Columbia—Design and construction—History. 7. Wooden boats—British Columbia—Design and construction—History. I. Title.
VM140.W28W34 2008   623.82'0092   C2008-904287-5

DEDICATION

This book is dedicated to my grandfather, Iver Wahl, whom I called Papa. Without his support of my project to collect the history of the family business, I doubt the research would have gone to the depth and breadth that it did.

He shared the first story with me in the summer of 2003 while I was visiting him and my grandmother, Mary, in Prince Rupert; the last story came in the fall of 2004, shortly before he passed away. He delivered some of the stories with so much passion that he caught me off guard—I had never seen that side of him before. I can only guess now that asking him to talk about the old days allowed him to relive an exciting past that was filled with many hardships—yet remembered fondly. The knowledge I gained from his stories is his legacy to me.

This photo of us was taken on my visit to Prince Rupert in the summer of 2004, when we had our last conversation together. He passed away at the age of eighty. Rest in peace, Papa.

The Ocean Roamer *coming into Departure Bay,*
Nanaimo. At 56 feet, it was probably the largest
wooden troller ever built on the BC coast.
COURTESY OF NORTH PACIFIC PAPERS, NORTH PACIFIC CANNERY
NHS, PORT EDWARD, BC

Prestige *was the sister seine boat to* Predator. *Both boats were built by Ernest Wahl at his Kent Street boat shop.* PHOTO COURTESY ROALD AND VIOLET WAHL.

CONTENTS

FOREWORD

By David Rahn
Publisher, *Western Mariner*

In the mid-twentieth century the West Coast fishing industry developed some classic wooden boat designs at a number of legendary boatyards, few of which were more highly esteemed than the Wahl family boatyard in Prince Rupert. Wahl boats set the standard by which fishermen judge all others. On the West Coast there is no higher praise for a commercial wooden boatbuilder than to have his work compared favourably to the Wahls'.

Wahl boats are graceful, lovely riding sea boats, functional as you could wish for; but fishermen love Wahl boats most for their beauty. You *want* to scrape and sand and renew the varnish and paint each season. You feel that you're entrusted with the care of a masterpiece and letting the finish run down to craze and crack cannot be considered. Your rewards are those perfect, endless days riding groundswells on the nearest thing to perfection in wood you and the seabirds will ever see. Brace in the cockpit, sight down the glistening gumwood rail-cap from the checkers to the bow and watch the hull gracefully rise to the waves and fall back gently as it was meant to do, and the memory of those moments will outlast all the fish you'll bring aboard.

These are wonderful ships, perfect for their place and time, and Ryan Wahl's book adds a new and lasting dimension to a family legacy that lives on in the memories of West Coast fishermen lucky enough to have put to sea in a Wahl boat.

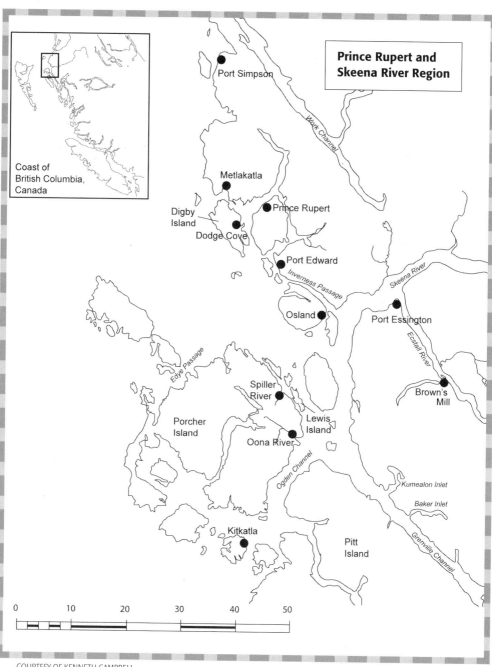

Prince Rupert and Skeena River Region

Coast of British Columbia, Canada

Port Simpson

Metlakatla

Prince Rupert

Digby Island

Dodge Cove

Port Edward

Osland

Port Essington

Work Channel

Inverness Passage

Skeena River

Ecstall River

Spiller River

Brown's Mill

Edye Passage

Porcher Island

Lewis Island

Oona River

Ogden Channel

Kumealon Inlet

Baker Inlet

Kitkatla

Pitt Island

Grenville Channel

0   10   20   30   40   50

COURTESY OF KENNETH CAMPBELL

The troller Loretta A, *built in the early 1960s for Joe Amstutz of Nanaimo, BC.*

NORTH PACIFIC PAPERS, NORTH PACIFIC CANNERY NHS, PORT EDWARD, BC

INTRODUCTION

For people not affected, the golden age of the commercial fishing industry in British Columbia has recently passed with little notice. Like logging, it was one of the engines that drove the BC economy and provided the seed for the creation of other industries and settlements along the entire BC coast.

As commercial fishing waned, most of the salmon canneries either shut down or significantly reduced production. Fishing supply stores now carry little for the commercial fisherman (though plenty for the recreational fisherman). Hardware stores have also discontinued or cut back much of what they used to stock for the sole benefit of commercial fishermen. But the one industry that has been completely eliminated by the decline of commercial fishing and the resulting reduction of the fishing fleet is the construction of wooden fishing vessels.

For three generations my family built wooden fishboats for the BC commercial fishing industry. In fishing and boat-building circles during that time span the name Wahl became synonymous with efficiency, quality and beauty. Its reputation led the Wahl family to have one of the most successful commercial boat-building enterprises on the BC coast.

I learned about the rise and fall of the family business mostly from my grandfather, Iver Wahl, one of six sons of Øystein (Ed) Wahl, a Norwegian immigrant who in his twenties left one rugged shoreline to explore new opportunities on another—the north coast of British Columbia.

It's not clear whether he stumbled into boat building because of its close ties to fishing or had been just waiting for the opportunity to get into it, but once he discovered his passion for it, there was no turning back, and his small Prince Rupert business gradually grew to an enterprise vital to the North Coast fishing industry.

This book began as a family history research project in the summer of 2003 while I was in Prince Rupert. I had been browsing through my grandmother Mary's scrapbook of articles relating to the family, and at some point I asked her if anyone had written the history of the family boat-building business. "No," she said and minutes later I found myself driving down to Radio Shack to purchase a tape recorder. Fuelled by a touch of anxiety at the thought of losing this important era in my family's history and even more by curiosity about what transpired during those days, I spent the remainder of my visit interviewing my grandparents.

From that experience I realized my grandfather's stories would be my strongest source of information, but when I got home the research really took off. I contacted people who had worked at the boatyards or were related to the Wahl family or their business. Oral histories from former employees were the most rewarding, as they offered invaluable insights into the personalities of my ancestors, at least half of whom had already passed away by the time I was born.

Almost as rewarding was reading articles on the family business in the pages of *Western Fisheries* magazine, which was published from the 1930s to the 1980s. In it was a regular column that provided updates on all the boatyards on the coast. The archives of both the city and region of Prince Rupert and the North Pacific Cannery Archives contain an abundance of photos and other documentation that proved very useful. I was lucky enough to obtain a ledger spanning five years of the post–World War II period that helped me significantly in understanding the state of production during that time. (Thanks, Eddie!) Current and former owners also provided many photos and stories of Wahl boats, and the internet was a great research and communication tool for tracking down information such as the early history of the family farm in Norway.

The more I researched these topics the more I felt compelled to set the single thread of the family's story into the larger context to give a greater understanding of why the wood construction of commercial fishing vessels ended. Thus, expanding the story to include other boat builders and the overall progression and decline of the wooden boat-building industry became natural phases of the research. However, the book doesn't cover how wooden boat building on this coast started. I do know that long before my great-grandfather set foot on North American soil in the early 1900s, trading that involved fish had been occurring between Native peoples and white men and that in time this trade evolved into a commercial fishery. The industry took a giant leap forward after the invention of a safe and viable canning process in the late 1800s, and after that its success and prosperity were predicated on a steady supply of fish. This led to boat shops being erected along the entire BC coast to create small and then larger and larger wooden boats for the fish canneries and private buyers. Ed Wahl became one of those boat builders, taking great pride in delivering boats that were strong and beautiful.

The Wahl commercial fishboats presented in this book are just a small fraction of those the three generations of the family built over a sixty-year span because very little in the way of documentation (ledgers, sales orders, etc.) remains and no formal count of the boats they built has been done. There is a consensus, however, that the boats number over one thousand and some informants have estimated the number as high as thirteen hundred, which seems reasonable if you include all three generations. With this many boats constructed and records scarce, I knew early in the research phase of this project that tracking down photos and details of all the Wahl boats in a reasonable time would be virtually impossible, but the hundred or so mentioned in this book are fine examples of Wahl design in their respective times.

I was only three years old when production at the original boatyard at Dodge Cove ceased and work was transferred to the family's Fairview Bay boatyard at Prince Rupert. A few years later the Dodge Cove Boatyard was sold and the new owner hired my grandfather as the master shipwright. Sadly, I have little memory of what took place on the main building floor as my attention was usually on the scrap lumber piled by the band saw, which provided me with the materials for the construction of toy boats. In 1989, however, I did see one more boat built. I was seventeen at the time and helped in the construction of my uncle's boat, the *Legacy*—the last Wahl boat built in wood.

Despite being stuck with grunt work such as sanding, looking back on those days I realize that in helping to build the *Legacy*, I developed a deep sense of connection to a significant era in my family's history. I have also come to appreciate wooden boats in general now, and today when I walk along the piers at a marina and look at the boats, I don't just see a graceful sheer line or a handsome wheelhouse. I also see a father in the stern teaching his son how to clean a fish, a mother and daughter hauling in the catch and the family dog barking at a fish flipping around in the pen. And seeing a poorly kept boat now makes my heart sink as I imagine all the times that boat brought the skipper's crew and family home safely.

This story of the contribution my great-grandfather and his descendants made to a craft that helped shaped modern boat building is something I am very proud of and I wanted to share it with more than just the family. I hope that you, like me, come to appreciate this relatively short and unique era in wooden boat building on the BC coast.

Three boatyards, three generations

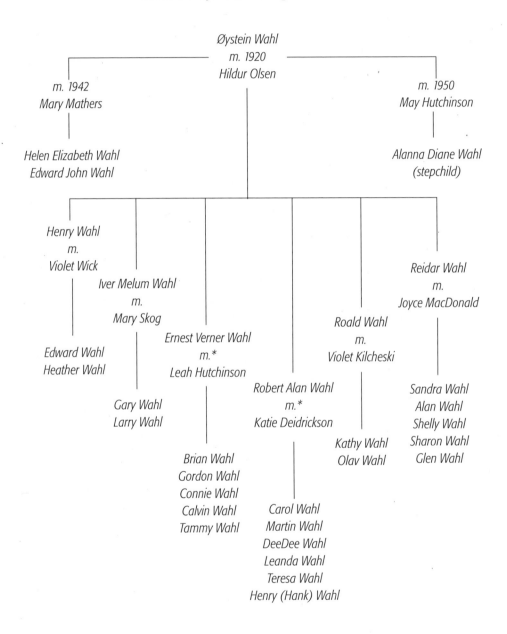

Øystein Wahl
m. 1920
Hildur Olsen

m. 1942
Mary Mathers

m. 1950
May Hutchinson

Helen Elizabeth Wahl
Edward John Wahl

Alanna Diane Wahl
(stepchild)

Henry Wahl
m.
Violet Wick

Reidar Wahl
m.
Joyce MacDonald

Iver Melum Wahl
m.
Mary Skog

Roald Wahl
m.
Violet Kilcheski

Edward Wahl
Heather Wahl

Ernest Verner Wahl
m.*
Leah Hutchinson

Gary Wahl
Larry Wahl

Robert Alan Wahl
m.*
Katie Deidrickson

Sandra Wahl
Alan Wahl
Shelly Wahl
Sharon Wahl
Glen Wahl

Kathy Wahl
Olav Wahl

Brian Wahl
Gordon Wahl
Connie Wahl
Calvin Wahl
Tammy Wahl

Carol Wahl
Martin Wahl
DeeDee Wahl
Leanda Wahl
Teresa Wahl
Henry (Hank) Wahl

*refers to first marriage only

CHAPTER ONE

THE LEGACY

And first with nicest skill and art,
Perfect and finished in every part,
A little model the Master wrought,
Which should be to the larger plan
What the child is to the man,
Its counterpart in miniature;

(From "The Building of the Ship"
by Henry Wadsworth Longfellow)

The launching of the *Legacy*, the last Wahl wooden fishing boat, at the former Wahl Boatyard on Dodge Cove in 1990 was a low-key affair despite what it represented to both the shipbuilding and fishing industries of British Columbia. It was one of the last—if not the last—commercial fishboat to be built completely of wood on this coast. But the diminishing ripples caused by the *Legacy* as it hit the water signified the unofficial end to the crafting of large wooden boats not only in the commercial industry but in the pleasure boat industry as well.

Seventy-five years before the *Legacy*'s launching, the man who started the Wahl boat-building enterprise had left his homeland, Norway, to make his fortune in the rich, resource-based industries on the west coast of North America. Øystein (Edward) Wahl was a robust nineteen-year-old when he boarded the twelve-hundred-passenger emigrant steamship *Bergensfjord* at the port of Bergen on March 3, 1915, bound for Ellis Island, New York. He had $25 dollars in his pocket.

From left: *Ed, a neighbour and Haldor on the* Namdal, *named for the district in Norway from which Ed and Haldor came. The photo was probably taken when the brothers were fishing in the Seattle area.* ANTON RAMFJORD JR. COLLECTION

If the measure of a man is how he faces challenges, the young Ed Wahl was high on the scale, but he had the advantage of his Viking heritage to draw on. He was born in a land of fearless hunters, warriors and explorers—the Viking explorer Leif Erikson had set foot in the New World five hundred years before Columbus voyaged west. More importantly, by continually travelling on the world's oceans and rivers, Ed Wahl's forebears had become not only expert navigators but highly adept and technical ship-builders as well. In fact, if it hadn't been for their superior shipbuilding skills, their distant voyages would not have been possible. Through hundreds of years of evolution, their ships developed into light but strong and extremely seaworthy vessels that were capable of feats unmatched by any other ship designs of their day.

But the young Ed Wahl was influenced by his Viking heritage as well as what was happening around him in those years prior to World War I. Emigration fever had hit Norway and the other northern European countries in the early 1800s and it continued for over a century, causing

From left: *a young Ed Wahl, unknown friend, Haldor Wahl.*
MARY WAHL COLLECTION

a steady population movement to the west by those in pursuit of greater freedom of religion, more money or adventure. A Wahl family member had left Norway for the United States around 1860 and Ed's older brother, Haldor, had already followed in his footsteps.

Ed Wahl was born on July 20, 1895, in Nærøy, Nord-Trøndelag, Norway, to Haldor Iversen Wahl and Mathilde Andreasdatter Juul. Farming and fishing were the two main occupations in Norway at that time—farming in the summer and fishing in winter for the cod that migrated down the Norwegian coast from the Barents Sea—and Ed Wahl's father was both fisherman and farmer. Ed, his three brothers and one sister grew up on a centuries-old family farm where their father grew grain and potatoes and raised cattle and poultry. Ed and his brother Haldor left school at fourteen to work on the farm and, as Ed reached manhood, he became both farmer and fisherman like his father, although on the side he also learned cabinet-making. This wasn't enough for him, however, and when his brother offered to pay his way to the United States, Ed happily accepted.

After arriving in New York, Ed took the train across the continent to the town of Everett, Washington, where Haldor was waiting for him. The two young men joined the commercial fishing fleet and for a short while plied the local waters, including Neah Bay on the northwestern tip of the Olympic Peninsula, before leaving for Alaska where they fished for dog salmon.

In 1920, with World War I finally over, Ed and Haldor took a temporary respite from North America and headed back home. While there, Ed married sixteen-year-old

Opposite: *Haldor Wahl as a lumberjack at Quathiaski Cove.*
ANTON RAMFJORD JR. COLLECTION

Hildur Olsen. The Olsen family had emigrated from Norway to Saskatchewan in 1910 but frequently made trips back to the old country, and their latest visit happened to coincide with that of the Wahl brothers. After a brief stay in Norway, the newlyweds and Haldor made their way to British Columbia's now familiar west coast and the two men took jobs logging at Quathiaski Cove on Quadra Island, an experience that resulted in Ed's becoming an exceptional saw filer. It was also at Quathiaski Cove that Ed and Hildur Wahl's first son was born in 1922. They named him Henry.

With his adventurous Viking spirit, Ed Wahl was always willing to move on if it would give him the opportunity to try something new. So it was about a year after Henry's birth that he set his sights on the north again, but this time his destination was not Alaska but Port Essington on the south bank of the Skeena River. Despite a decline in the economy in that area due to the end of the steamboat era, the little town seemed to have great possibilities. Ed bought a 6-hp, gas-engined, 27-foot gillnet boat named *Viking*, with which he planned to fish on the Skeena. He converted the stern into living quarters by removing the drum and setting up a tent in its place. Joining his small family for this new adventure were Hildur's parents, who bunked in the wheelhouse for the trip. They set off up the coast on the days-long journey to their new home, the last major move that Ed Wahl would make.

When the Wahls arrived in Port Essington in 1923, the town had three canneries and more dotted the shores of Inverness Passage and the Skeena River. But the first thing Ed discovered was that a Fisheries Department law prohibited gas-powered boats from fishing on the river. The standard Skeena fishboat at the time was the Columbia River model, a two-man, round-bottomed, double-ended sailboat of up to 26 feet. Locomotion was by oar or sail, and setting and hauling the nets was all done by hand. A gas-powered cannery tugboat towed these boats to and from the fishing grounds. Although Ed was forced to tie the *Viking* up for that season, fortunately the prohibition on gas-powered boats was lifted the following year and he made history by becoming the first fisherman to use a gas-powered boat on the river. Other fishermen followed suit and in a few years the last sailboat was gone, ending that era in BC commercial fishing.

In the same year that Ed began fishing on the Skeena, for reasons his family could not later explain—though additional income in the off-season would seem to have been a good motive—the former cabinetmaker decided to pick up a hammer again. But this time he wouldn't be

The families of Ed and Haldor Wahl at Dodge Cove. Back row (left to right) Ed Wahl, Hildur Wahl, Sigrid Wahl (Haldor's wife), Haldor Wahl, Ernest Wahl, Bobby Wahl. Middle row (left to right): Howard Wahl (Haldor's oldest son), female family friend, Henry Wahl. Front row (left to right): Erling Wahl (Haldor's youngest son), Steinar Wahl (Haldor's second-oldest son), Roald Wahl, Reidar Wahl. Missing from photo: Iver Wahl.

crafting cabinet doors or taking on other small wood-working projects. His intention was grander—he would build a commercial fishboat.

It is said that fishermen make the best shipwrights and, as his Viking ancestors had done before him, Ed Wahl used the knowledge gained by his years of fishing and learning how boats perform on water to guide him in designing a seaworthy boat. When he set out to lay his first keel, his goal was not only to build a boat that would perform well but also to give it lines that were just as flowing as the medium it floated on. Water-shedding flares at the bow, a handsomely crafted wheelhouse, graceful sheer lines ending in a sturdy, super buoyant stern—these were all components of his vision and would in time become the trademarks of Wahl boats, trademarks that allowed them to stand out from the rest of the fleet. Ed Wahl's first boats, however, didn't look like this. At the beginning of his boat-building career, his designs were like that of any other builder—narrow in the beam, straight sheer lines and simple box-shaped cabins. "Build 'em sleek and slender" was the general boat-building rule then, based on the principle that the less resistance the boat offered the faster it could cruise.

With his specialty in joinery, Ed was already adept at preparing wood and assembling it in an efficient and cohesive fashion. But unlike his Viking ancestors who had used a construction technique called clinker (also known as lapstrake), in which the planks overlap each other at the edges to form a shell, to build his first boat Ed chose the carvel technique, laying the planks edge to edge over a frame to form a smooth hull surface. Although carvel had originated in the Mediterranean—it was used most

Opposite: *Ed Wahl in the stern of his boat, the* Reward I.
MARY WAHL COLLECTION

notably in the construction of Columbus's *Niña*, *Pinta* and *Santa Maria*—this style had gradually moved northward until by the 1800s it had become the dominant shipbuilding technique in Norway. The carvel style was also preferred over the clinker style in British Columbia because it allowed for more flexibility in design, faster construction and a stronger hull, as well as easier repairs. Clinker building, however, remained popular for small vessels, including rowboats.

Before Ed could start work, he needed a boat shop and fortunately right at this time one became available at the south end of Port Essington. It was a modest shed but big enough to house a 32-foot boat. That winter he started teaching himself the craft of boat construction and, like the builders of centuries past, he did not rely on plans or blueprints. Instead, he combined memory and experience with rules of thumb in practical boat design. To start the process, he transposed his vision onto a "half-model"—a one-inch to one-foot scale version of the full-sized boat—but only one-half of it. With this miniature to guide him throughout the rest of the construction process he could build "by eye"—a skill that the traditional master shipwrights had developed thousands of years before the creation of the blueprint. Rather than tediously measuring the dimensions of each piece of wood required, they would look at the model, estimate the shape and cut it without the aid of a measuring device.

The following spring Ed dragged the 32-foot double-ender *Nornan* down the beach to launch it into the Skeena. The boat was designed to be a gillnetter, but as my grandfather Iver Wahl later commented, it also proved itself as a halibut boat when Ed caught a four-hundred-pounder with it. At the end of that fishing season he sold the boat and that winter got busy in the shop on his next

Boat Types

The commercial fishboats built by the Wahls fall into five types: gill-netters, trollers, longliners, seiners and packers. The types are differentiated by how they catch the fish: **gillnetters** set a net in a long straight line that hangs from the water surface like an invisible curtain, entangling the fish by the gills; **trollers** slowly drag numerous lines with hooks through the water; **longliners** set a long line which is anchored to the ocean floor at each end, catching fish with baited hooks attached to it; **seiners** set a net in a circle that forms a bag when hauled in, trapping the fish. Packer boats don't catch fish but rather transport fish from the fishing grounds to the canneries for delivery and then processing.

Gillnetters are usually the smallest boats in the fleet (30-38 feet), followed by trollers and longliners (38-60 feet), and finally seiners (50-80 feet).

Gillnetters, trollers and seiners catch salmon, while longliners catch bottom fish, primarily halibut and cod.

Parts of a Fishing Boat

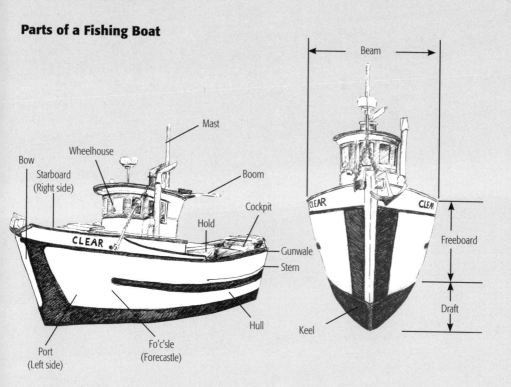

ILLUSTRATION BY TIA MCLENNAN

one. Over the next four years he continued the routine of fishing the new boat in the summer, selling it at the end of season and building another one in the winter.

The operation was small enough that Ed could manage it himself, although when he was putting in the ribs and fastening the planks to the frame, he would sometimes call Hildur into the shop to lend a hand. Hildur had a very busy life as well. While living in Port Essington she bore three more sons: Iver Melum on July 29, 1924, Ernest Verner on November 17, 1925, and Robert "Bobby" Alan three years later. Hildur's mother, Mathilda, served as a midwife for Bobby's delivery.

CHAPTER TWO

A NEW BOATYARD,
A NEW START

B oat building had proved to be a successful side business for Ed Wahl, but by the late 1920s he was trying to find a way to expand it. This led him to move away from Port Essington in search of a

Dodge Cove in the late 1930s or early 1940s. On the left, Dodge Island (better known as Hospital Island) sits on the harbour border. Between it and the point on the right is the cove entrance through which Prince Rupert can be seen. To the left is the wooden walkway to the wharf. MARY WAHL COLLECTION

place that could accommodate his burgeoning enterprise. In 1928 he moved his family briefly to Prince Rupert and a year later to Dodge Cove, a small fishing village tucked away on Digby Island, a short boat ride west of Prince Rupert. Barely settled at the time, Dodge Cove afforded plenty of space and the perfect landscape to see his long-term dreams fulfilled.

I n 1912 in anticipation of the population boom expected after the completion of the Grand Trunk Pacific Railway, the government built a three-storey quarantine hospital on Hospital Island to isolate patients with communicable diseases. No penny was spared in the construction of the hospital, staff accommodations and a marine station around the corner to the south. The Grand Trunk Pacific went into receivership in 1914, however, and the story goes that the hospital had only one patient, a sailor who was suffering from a bad cold. In the 1930s it served as the residence for the families working at the marine station and in the 1970s it became the headquarters for archaeologists digging in the area. Picnickers began coming to the island shortly after the hospital closed. Visible in the photo, to the right of the island, is a 672-foot-long wooden bridge that once connected Hospital Island to Digby Island. At the other end of the bridge is the house built for the quarantine hospital's physician and his family.

Hospital Island in 1916.
COURTESY OF THE WRATHALL COLLECTION, PRINCE RUPERT CITY & REGIONAL ARCHIVES AND MUSEUM OF NORTHERN BC

When Ed moved to Dodge Cove, his brother Haldor
followed suit, bringing with him his wife, Sigrid, who,
like Hildur, had come over from the old country. Haldor
was by this time making a good living as a halibut fisherman on his boat the *Domino II.* To save costs on a home
for Haldor and his family, he and Ed bought a house in
Anyox, a company mining town on Observatory Inlet,
about eighty miles north of Prince Rupert. They disman-
tled the house, brought it down to Dodge Cove on a scow
and reassembled it on a lot across the road from Ed's boatyard. In that house, Haldor and Sigrid raised their own
boys—Howard, Steinar and Erling.

In August of 1930 Ed and Hildur welcomed twin
boys, Roald and Reidar, to their own brood, making six

*The north end of Dodge Cove where the boatyard (close to centre) and the
Wahl family homes were located. On the right is teardrop-shaped Hospital
Island.* ED AND DIANE WAHL COLLECTION

A Wahl family photo, c. 1935. Back row (left to right): *Ernest, Henry, Bobby, Iver;* middle row: *Hildur, Reidar, Ed;* front row: *Roald.* MARY WAHL COLLECTION

Left to right: *Roald, Hildur and Reidar.* "Mother wanted a girl so bad that when Reidar and I came along they kept my hair long," Roald said.

ERNEST AND KAY WAHL COLLECTION

boys to follow in their father's footsteps. Ernest recalled that "the twins were born in Rupert. I remember when they were born. That was the first time they had to get a doctor for one of us kids. The midwife didn't know it was twins. So here the first one was born and then she said to Dad, 'Ed, you better get the doctor. There's another one coming!'"

When Ed and Haldor arrived with their families in Dodge Cove, it probably felt like home. Norwegian fishermen had started to settle the area in the early 1900s, carving a community out of the wilderness, and as a result their settlement had become known locally as the "Norwegian Village." By 1938 there were forty homes

Digby Island was named after Henry Almarus Digby, a second lieutenant on HMS *Malacca* during the 1870s. Dodge Cove, about halfway down the island's eastern shoreline, was named in 1906 after George B. Dodge, who surveyed the Prince Rupert harbour. For many decades Dodge Cove has been a favourite spot for archaeologists seeking artifacts left by the Tsimshian people whose villages once dotted the shores of Digby Island and the western shore of Kaien Island.

there and the population eventually peaked and levelled out at about one hundred people. The settlement had no general store so all groceries had to be brought from town. Helen Iverson, Hildur Wahl's niece, would later comment that "the only time people had to venture into [Prince] Rupert was to buy groceries and give birth!" The damp climate and muskeg-like soil limited what vegetables could be grown there, but the conditions were favourable for potatoes and in the early years the residents bought theirs from a hermit named Potato Oscar who lived just down from Dodge Cove. The story goes that he disappeared during World War II and nobody knows what happened to him.

The Wahl brothers' move to Dodge Cove occurred just before the Great Depression, when western Canada was especially hard hit due to rapidly falling prices for natural resources. The residents of Dodge Cove were not immune to its effects, but a strong community support system helped them to survive it. Compared to his neighbours, however, Ed was doing quite well. He had a beautiful new house and two sources of income that gave him the means to maintain a decent lifestyle. After buying the essential items, he had money left over to buy tools and equipment for the boat shop and materials to expand it. "[The Depression] affected a lot of people on Digby Island," Iver said, "but it didn't affect Dad as he always had enough work. We were lucky. We were really lucky. We were what you might call wealthy. We had lots of clothes because our mother was a wonderful seamstress. We always had food … [Dad would go] to Burns Meat Market and buy half a cow. He salted that and cut it up in chunks and pounded it up and dried it. Dried beef. Dried salted beef … I can still taste it. And deer meat … he never missed hunting. Dad and his brother always went together

In total, three schoolhouses have existed in Dodge Cove. The first was built in 1933 when there were finally enough children to warrant the provincial government supplying a teacher, but classes were provided only up to grade seven or eight. When this original building was torn down, Ed Wahl organized and supervised the construction of a new one, even making the blackboard himself. By the time I was old enough to go to grade school in the late 1970s, the last schoolhouse had been closed and the Dodge Cove children had to take a ferry to Prince Rupert to attend school.

The first schoolhouse (left) *and the second, much larger schoolhouse* (below).
MARY WAHL COLLECTION

and he never came home until he had six deer." Besides
salmon and halibut, herring that had been salted down in
tubs was another big part of the family's winter diet. "If
we had a little bit too much food, Dad always gave it to
the neighbours. He put them to work whenever he could.
If he didn't put them to work in the shed, he put them to
work around the property—on the stumps, you know."

Ed Wahl's Dodge Cove Boatyard was initially run as
a family business, although at times he hired neighbours
or Hildur's brothers, Otto and Ole Olsen, at fifty cents
an hour. And as she had done when they had their first
boatshed in Port Essington, Hildur also helped out. But in
time Ed's biggest help would come from his sons.

In the years before they began working in the boatyard, the young Wahl boys were like any other children
of their time. With no radio or television, they were
forced to entertain themselves by using their surround-
ings and a little imagination. Their main enjoyment came
from building model boats out of scrap wood found in
the boatyard. After sifting through the scrap piles to find
good pieces, they cut them to the right shape and, by
mimicking the steps their father took to build a real boat,
they crafted the pieces into elaborate models up to five
feet in length. With such attention to the tiniest detail, the
boats caught the attention of visitors to the Cove. "We
were always making boats," Iver recalled. "People used
to come over [to the island on] Sundays for picnics and
when they spotted our boats on the beach they got all
excited. Then they bought them from us."

As the boys matured, building models became less satis-
fying and they decided to scale up construction and get
into rowboat building. Once they had a contest to see who
could finish first. "Ernest, he got his finished," Iver said.
"He did a really nice job of it. Henry and I, we got stuck

with our pants down. We only got ours half done. I got mine ribbed and Henry—I think he got his half planked. But then we had to go work in the [boat]shed and that was the end of that. Our play boat days were over."

As soon as his sons were strong enough to keep up a decent pace, Ed started them on light duties such as sweeping the floors, getting wood for the steambox and creosoting the insides of the boats. "Your grandpa Iver and I started about the same time," Ernest told me. "Dad was always busy, busy, busy. Us kids used to work all the time. [We were] sweeping floors and keeping the fire going. Anyway, I puttied so many nail holes I could do it in my sleep." As they got older and stronger, they advanced to more laborious and technical tasks. By 1932, as there was as yet no schoolhouse in Dodge Cove, the two oldest boys, Henry (aged ten) and Iver (aged eight) were working with their dad for about half of each day. By this time Henry was strong enough to hold onto the end of a plank.

When the younger boys began working in the shop, they followed the same apprenticeship as their older brothers—starting out with simple shop and boat duties and then focussing on such critical and difficult boat-building steps as planking, caulking and puttying the nail holes. All the boys had a keen interest in the work and, after learning one aspect of the job, they moved to another and another until they had finally learned it all. "By fourteen we were planking," said Ernest. "In the wintertime my hands were so cold they were stiff. We didn't mind if we were on the steambox."

An important part of the boys' boat-building apprenticeship time was spent learning the characteristics of each species of wood and where and how they were used in a boat. The framing, for example, was made entirely of oak, a hardwood that under extreme heat can be bent into the shape of the hull. For planking, cedar and fir were the best choices because of their high resistance to rot. Western red cedar, a very durable wood, is particularly valued in boat building for its flexibility. It is a prominent species in West Coast forests and Native peoples used it extensively

Students in a Dodge Cove school photo from the late 1930s. Back row (left to right): *Ernest Wahl, Harry Olsen (Hildur Wahl's nephew), Eva Simondson (Hildur Wahl's niece), Doris Olsen, Lenny Hadland, Bobby Wahl;* second to back row: *Roald Wahl, Lenny Olsen, Dolly Simondson;* middle row: *Odd Eidsvik, Ray Lund, Jerry Melin;* front row: *Reidar Wahl, Donny Olsen, Harold Eidsvik, Anita Hadland.* ROALD AND VIOLET WAHL COLLECTION

in making dugout canoes. Boat lumber also has to be free of large knots and cut edge-grain, that is, with the wood grain running the length of the board, as this gives it great flexibility. In contrast, a board that is cut cross-grain won't bend enough for boat building, even in the extreme heat of a steambox.

Ed also taught his sons the heart of the master ship-wright's skill—cutting by eye. Each plank, for example, had to be cut with a curve that matched the shape of the hull in that particular spot. He taught his boys how to do it just by looking at where the plank had to go and making a mental image of the shape. While holding onto that image, they would walk over to the band saw and cut the shape out. It took them years and years of practice to acquire this particular skill, but the more time they spent doing it the better at it they became. Eventually it was second nature to all of them—as easy as it is for the rest of us to tie our shoes—although the two oldest boys, Henry and Iver, were particularly good at it. The only measuring they had to do was at the top of the hull when cutting for the sheer line. This skill saved an enormous amount of time and further streamlined the Wahls' boat-building process.

Another important lesson the boys learned from their father was not wasting lumber. The planking, for example, was cut from each board like the pieces of a jigsaw puzzle. Doing so was a challenge, but Ed was adamant that it be done and the boys turned it into a game, guessing how many planks they could get out of each board. "You could just about tell by looking at the board how much you could get out of it," Iver told me. "That was the inter-esting part ... and that way, by the end of the day you didn't have a bunch of rubbish for the junk pile. The less lumber you use the more [money] in your pocket."

Although a school was built in Dodge Cove in 1933, like many young people during the Depression years, the Wahl boys soon had to forgo the classroom to help run the family business as there was no money to hire outside labour. And like their father who had been forced to leave school at fourteen to work on the farm, once they began working full-time in the boatyard, they never went back to complete their formal education.

Leaving school and working in the boatyard at such a young age wasn't a choice the boys were given, but despite that, Iver remembers those early days with fondness as he and his brothers always enjoyed working with their father. "Dad, he wasn't a slave driver. We wanted to be with him anyhow." The apprenticeship was long and arduous and, with the amount of time the boys spent together at the boatyard, a strong brotherhood formed between them. But given that closeness, not surprisingly arguments occurred now and then.

"You have a little scrap once in a while," Iver said. "We were all that way. If you don't ... then something's wrong. Henry and I had a room upstairs in our house with a bunk on each side of it. I remember when quitting time came around, we sprawled out in our bunks. We had some helluva fights up there. At night we used to start a wrestling match and then Mom and Dad would get all the other kids to be quiet and sit around. And Dad, he got the biggest kick out of it. He really liked it. A real show for him, I guess. Dad always stuck up for me because I was the smallest one. But for a while there, you know, I was stronger than Henry—I was built pretty good—and I got Henry so mad that he used to cry. He didn't like me beating him because I was younger than him. All considering, though, we've been together all these years and we got along the way we should. We had great respect for each other and we always had to know where [the others] were at all times. You always think of the worst things."

Building Up the Business

When Ed started boat building, power tools didn't exist so every aspect of the job—cutting, planing, sanding and drilling—was carried out by human power. In the early 1930s, however, he managed to save up for his first gas-powered piece of equipment: a large band saw powered by a 5-hp Fairbanks-Morse engine. The piston of the single cylinder sat horizontally with a flywheel on each side. The benefits of the gas-powered band saw were immediately apparent to him and paved the way for more gas-powered equipment. Next came a planer/joiner powered by a 490 Chevy car engine that Ed bought for $100 from a garage in town. An edger with a 5-hp Vivian engine and two more gas-powered band saws, as well as a small portable band saw, soon found their way into the boat shop. Keeping all the gas tanks full was a new task that came with this modernization and the whole crew shared in this duty.

During the 1930s construction at the Wahl Boatyard was limited to trollers and halibut boats since the Japanese builders in the area were filling the canneries' requirements for gillnet boats. By this time Ed was building two 37-foot trollers a year, selling one and keeping the other to fish the next season. At the end of the fishing season, he would sell that boat and build two more, again selling one and keeping the other. Each of these trollers, which he sold for $650, went out with rigging, rudder, tanks and the wood for the mast and boom. "I remember the *Real* that was built over on Digby," Ed's son Ernest said. "That was one of the first ones. And the *Fram* ... yeah, that would

Ed atop the first boat out of the Wahl Boatyard on Dodge Cove. He built the troller Fram *(which means "forward" in Norwegian) for himself.*
ANTON RAMFJORD JR. COLLECTION

have been the first one and then came the *Real*. [The *Fram* was built in 1930, the *Real* in 1931.] I remember the *Real* was brought in to have some work done when it was forty years old. We said to Dad that we should think about recaulking this boat and Dad said, 'Why, is it leaking?' 'I can check and see,' I said. So I checked the seams and they still had the red lead putty in there and the cotton was still snow white. I can still see those nice, fine seams in that boat." Then he added, "The *Twilight* was another one that he built and sold the next year. That was the first boat I went fishing on."

Ed's system of fishing with a new boat each season was a major part of making sure his designs delivered the performance he expected. Testing the hull was critical. The shape had to meet adequate performance levels in stability, seaworthiness, sea-kindliness and speed—and also have lines he was happy with. Length, width, depth and weight in conjunction with the horsepower of the marine engines he installed were the important factors in achieving a well-designed boat and were, therefore, all considerations with which Ed and other shipwrights had to contend. Taking a boat out that he had built the previous winter gave him the chance to find and correct weak spots. The next winter he would alter the design and test it again on the fishing grounds the following spring. This cycle of designing, building, fishing and monitoring his boats carried on over many years until he had a baseline design he was happy with. After that, improvements relied less on testing and more on the experience that he had gained up to that point.

In the mid-1930s Ed extended the shop to start building 40-footers. One such boat was the 44-foot *Navigator H*, sold in 1938 for $1,100 to a Finlander named John Oppola.

Haldor Wahl and his family (excluding the boy on the right) as they leave British Columbia's north coast for Norway. ANTON RAMFJORD JR. COLLECTION

In the last years of the Depression, even as Ed's boat-building business was finally gaining a firm footing in the fishing community, he suffered two personal losses. In 1938 a request came from his parents for one of the brothers to come back to Norway to help on the family farm. Haldor, who had been very successful in the BC fishing industry and had both a home and family here, was as firmly planted on the North Coast as Ed was, but when Ed refused to return to Norway, the pressure increased on Haldor to go back. Sigrid, who was noticeably homesick, also put pressure on him. "She was sick most of the time over here—sick for the old country, I think," Iver said. "And they wanted him in the worst way to take over the farm, too." So at the end of the fishing season in 1938, Haldor and his family headed back to Norway. "Haldor had great hopes of coming back again once he got them all established over there," Iver said, "but then the war broke out and that was the end of that. He got stuck over there."

In 1939 the Depression ended as Canada geared up for World War II, but in that same year Hildur Marie Wahl died. A petite woman with a dark complexion, reddish hair and deep brown eyes, she was, according to people who knew her, a happy person, frequently singing at the top of her lungs and pleasing everyone with her beau-

Reward I. Ed built this 45-foot troller for himself shortly after Hildur died. It was probably the biggest boat to come out of the boatyard up to that point. He took it out trolling in the summer and, when things became too busy in the shop, he had other captains take it out for him on the halibut fishery. He kept it for three or fours years before selling it. ROALD AND VIOLET WAHL COLLECTION

tiful voice. Everyone around her knew that she was the rock of the family, keeping her husband and sons in line and running her household like "an old-country woman." And this was how she lived every day of her life until May 22, 1939, when she was hit with severe stomach pains. It was appendicitis and caused her death the following day. She was just thirty-five years old.

This was a very difficult time for Ed, not only because his wife had died but because he had to figure out how to take care of the six boys—the twins were just eight years old—and run his business at the same time. His only option was to pull Henry and Iver out of school. Iver told me, "I was nine years old when I started school but I had to quit when I was fifteen because my mother died. I helped with the house and took care of my younger brothers until Dad got a housekeeper."

The housekeeper Ed hired was nineteen-year-old Hilda Hadland, whose father, Julius, had established a sawmill at Oona River in 1921. Ed was so desperate for help that he pressed Hilda to convince her to take the job. "I was out in Oona River holidaying," Hilda said. "It was Christmastime and a friend of mine came out and said he had orders from Ed Wahl to bring me back to Digby. And he told me that they wanted me to cook for Ed and his six sons and I said, 'No way, no way! I'm not going to take that on!' Then I got another message [asking me to] just come and talk to him, so I went. I remember sitting down at the dining room table and listening to their 'persuasion'—oh, I wouldn't have to do this, I wouldn't have to do that—all the things that I wouldn't have to do. Well, finally I decided okay. I got $25 a month.

"The twins were so cute. I remember bathing them in the round washtub in the kitchen. They had their bedroom right beside the pantry—you had to walk through their bedroom to get to the pantry. They had a little bed that Ed had made. It was wide but quite short. At night they would sneak into the pantry and get into the cookies and canned prunes. Later you would see crumbs in their bed and prune pits under it.

"I had to wash the clothes by hand. Ernest was so good—he carried in the water for me. He would also see to it that the tank for the oil stove was filled. Bobby, he looked after himself. He was eleven at the time. Henry was very quick motioned and very high-strung. He'd come into the house I don't know how many times—you know, during the week—with his fingers bleeding. I don't know many times I bandaged up those fingers."

CHAPTER THREE

A BOAT A WEEK: THE HEYDAY OF WORLD WAR II

I t would take the start of World War II in September 1939 for Canada's economy to begin its recovery from the Depression years. Unemployment waned as men enlisted in the military and demand from overseas for Canada's raw materials rose. Prince Rupert, which became a strategic military post for both Canada and the United States, prospered more than ever before as thousands of troops from the Canadian and US armies poured into the little town, causing an unprecedented level of new construction in the town and along the waterfront.

Along with the armies, the canneries that lined Inverness Passage and the Skeena River also went to war. They included the Cassiar, Sunnyside (owned by BC Packers), Inverness, Oceanic (owned by Canadian Fishing Company) and Carlisle canneries, as well as Nelson Bros. Fisheries in Port Edward and the North Pacific Cannery (owned by the Anglo-British Columbia Packing Company). Many of them had been forced to close during the Depression, but now they were put back into action to meet the huge overseas demand for inexpensive and non-perishable protein foods. This new demand also forced the cannery managers to revitalize their aging gillnet fleets.

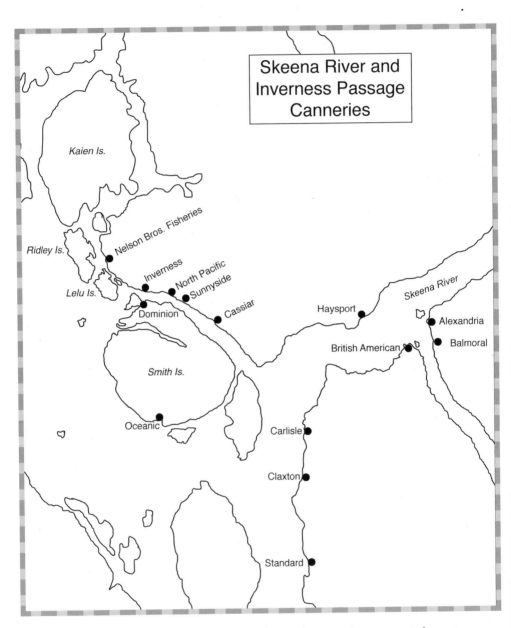

The canneries located along the Skeena River and Inverness Passage, most of which were customers of Wahl Boatyard. KENNETH CAMPBELL

By the time Ed Wahl had arrived in Port Essington in 1923, the canneries were purchasing all their gillnetters from the independent Japanese Canadian boat builders who dominated the industry on the North Coast. Men of great skill and craftsmanship, most of them had come to Canada before World War I and set up shop in Port Essington, Osland and Prince Rupert, where they had built huge fleets of gillnet sailboats for the local canneries. After sailboats were phased out of the fishing industry in the mid-1920s, these builders had converted the gillnet sailboats to accommodate gas engines and built new fleets of gas-powered gillnetters. The canneries employed other Japanese workers to make more boats and maintain the cannery fleets, but when World War II broke out, despite working frantically these crews simply didn't have the capacity to meet the huge demand for new boats. As a result, the canneries sent out bids to the local boatyards and many of them turned to Ed Wahl to build boats for them, although the North Pacific Cannery was his biggest customer.

The standard cannery gillnet boat launched out of the Wahl Boatyard at the beginning of World War II was between 30 feet and 32 feet long. The same basic mould was used for all of them and the length depended on where they would be fishing: 30 feet for the Skeena River, 31 feet for the mouth of the Skeena and 32 feet outside the river and for all rougher coastal waters. With a hull constructed

Malcolm Elder: "When Ed first started building gillnetters, the double-ender was the traditional way of building them, but some were special ordered to be a round stern. They came up with several different types and they changed the sterns a lot, but the bow remained pretty well the same."

Right: *A gillnetter lineup at the North Pacific Cannery. The Wahl boat is second from the right.*
COURTESY NORTH PACIFIC PAPERS, NORTH PACIFIC CANNERY NHS, PORT EDWARD, BC

Below: *The gillnetters were launched out of the boatyard by placing them on piping and then rolling them along until they hit the water.*
ROALD AND VIOLET COLLECTION

out of western redcedar, the Wahl gillnetters were light, sturdy and functional. The pilothouse had only enough room for the captain to stand and steer. Downstairs, the fo'c'sle (or forecastle) was built with the bare minimum of living accommodations and sleeping quarters. Aside from the two bunks that filled the front section, there was just enough space for a small marine oil stove, a countertop with a wash basin, locker seats and cupboards. All wood-work was roughed in by general carpenters and then finishing carpenters completed the work. These cannery gillnetters fetched the boatyard about $650 each, a very fair price at the time.

Nineteen-year-old Harold Johnson left Saskatchewan in June 1939 to visit his mother, Agnes Olsen, the elder sister of Hildur Wahl. "My mom and dad split up when I was about five or six years old," Harold said. "The Wahls had the old house right above the boat shop [at that time] and right next door was my mom and step-dad. Here also were all my cousins and aunts and uncles, and it was great to be among all these relatives. I went fishing for the season and then I worked for the railroad for a few months. When I came back, Ed needed help in the boat shop so I started wood-working for him." Harold's first duties were ribbing and planking and then he moved on to rough carpentry of the bunks, cupboards, wheelhouses and trunk cabins, as well as making engine beds. With Ed as his mentor Harold learned quickly. "I'd go fishing in the summers again for a couple of months and then I'd head back to the boat shop. When the war came on, then of course, he was really hiring. He must have had a crew of twenty-five people there, you know. Or twenty at least, I think."

Although Harold enjoyed his time boat building, his fondest memories are of activities that took place outside the boat-yard, such as the routine outings to town on Saturdays to get groceries and supplies for the shop. The crew member who was "lucky enough to get a turn" took the company boat to Prince Rupert to get hard-ware and supplies for the boatyard, as well as groceries for the crew. "We worked fast, ate fast and slept fast. Everything was full speed. As a break from that, Ed would get all us young guys onto a bigger boat—I think it was the *Reward*—and go around by Philpot to a loading platform. We'd have to pack and load that whole boat up. That was sort of a holiday for us. It was usually in the middle of a nice day 'cause you didn't want to get it all soaking wet in the rain. I really enjoyed that. And another thing I recall is the time—it was sort of a slack time in the summer—Ed grubbed up the same boat and loaded it up with gas and water and whatever. He took it up to Dundas and we went into this one big bay where the driftwood was all piled up—mostly cedar. We spent a day or two in there

The gillnetters were typically delivered to the canneries as shells and the canneries' own service crews would install the engines—the popular ones being Easthope and Vivian—and the shafts, propellers, steering and rigging. In a crunch, the canneries would ask the Wahls for help installing the engines. "A couple or three times," Ernest recalled, "Bob and I went up and installed all the engines and everything in those gillnetters—the last two or three boats. They had their own crew but they had to get them out for the season opening. Bob and I took one boat and their crew would be on another. In those days there was just the motor, drum, shaft and propeller. They had their

Harold and Hilda Johnson at their home in Parksville on Vancouver Island in 2004. RYAN WAHL COLLECTION

Harold Johnson married Ed's house-keeper, Hilda Hadland, in 1942 and they moved to Prince Rupert and started a family. Three years later Hilda returned to work briefly for the Wahls, but this time she had two more mouths to feed as two hired hands were living with the family. Again, she was putting three square meals on the table, mainly fish, vegetables and potatoes. Lunch was served at exactly twelve o'clock and by half past the men had returned to work in the boat shop.

Harold, meanwhile, had been lured back to the shop. "Once when it was slack, they talked me into coming back for maybe a month or two in the summertime. I had my little boat at the float and I would work in the daytime and then sleep on my boat." Eventually he left the boat shop and started in residential construction, where he stayed for the next fourteen years.

hauling them off the beach, jacking them up so we could roll them down. We rafted them together with line and towed them into Digby to the sawmill. It was a great outing. I was the cook and I can remember making French toast."

own machine shop where they made the shafts and everything. We installed the engine and everything in about fourteen hours." The life expectancy of these boats was about ten years, but with regular maintenance they could conceivably last much beyond that.

With the significant increase in business, Ed was forced to expand his operation and he hired about twenty more men, some of whom were military personnel stationed in Prince Rupert. It was apparent immediately, however, that a major expansion of the shed was needed, but instead of tacking on additions, tearing the old shed down and replacing it with a new and improved one made more sense. A crew was hired for the job and, to minimize disruption to boatyard operations, they built the new shed on top of the existing one. When time permitted, the Wahls also helped out a bit on the new shed and for a week Henry and Iver went out to John Group's mill at Oona River, twenty-five miles south of Prince Rupert (about a four-hour boat ride) to help cut the lumber for it.

Vidar Sandhals, whose mother was Hildur Wahl's cousin, recalls helping to put the shake roof on the new shed. "I remember telling them I knew where there was a good place to get cedar for shakes down the coast aways where we used to go deer hunting. There was a big cedar log on the beach—cedar stays good for ages—and it was sort of split in half. 'Why don't we go down and have a look?' I said, so we took a boat and [the log] was still there. We towed it home and sawed it up and made enough shakes for the roof."

On the south end of the new shed was a building floor big enough for the construction of two gillnetters or one larger boat. This floor sloped down toward the ocean to facilitate launching. The shed also had stalls where boats rested on wooden platforms—often referred

A nother family member who worked in the boat shop for a brief time was Vidar Sandhals. As Vidar remembers it, one winter in the early 1940s he opted not to go herring fishing and took a job at the Wahl Boatyard instead. He got hired on the way most did—by just showing up at the shop and asking for work. "They were building boats and needed somebody who could drive a nail, I guess. Things were pretty busy," Vidar said. "Ed did all the critical work. He shaped the planks and the rest of us would steam them and then nail them into place. I did a little bit of everything, including decking and putting in ribs. We all dug in there and had more work than we could do in a day. They taught you in a hurry. Henry and Iver were hard workers and you just tried to keep up to them. They were experts, of course, and we were learning. They did a lot of maintenance work, too—boats needing renailing or whatever— and at the same time they were improving the shop."

to as grids—to receive upper construction or bottom servicing, including copper painting. A detached stall on the north side provided an additional area for servicing and upper construction. Also expanding the boatyard's servicing capability was the addition of a cradle (also called carriage or ways) designed to go back and forth on a short railway that went down into the water; this set-up allowed the cradle to slide under a boat, scoop it up and bring it into the shed. The cradle, powered by a 120-hp, 6-cylinder Nash engine, could accommodate boats up to 55 feet in length and carry a maximum weight of about a hundred tons.

Assembly-Line Construction

The only way the Wahl Boatyard could deliver gillnet boats by the deadlines set by the canneries was to implement an assembly-line method of construction. The system that Ed worked out was a three-stage process. The keel for a new boat was laid on the main building floor and, after the basic construction of the hull was complete, that boat was moved ahead so that the keel for the next one could be laid in the now vacant spot behind it. The hull of the first boat was finished and painted before it was launched at high tide and checked for leaks. It was then brought back into one of the stalls or the cradle to receive its upper construction. The main tasks at this stage were the installation of the decking and construction of the trunk cabin and wheelhouse. Once this was complete, the boat was launched again for delivery to the cannery. There were variations in this system. For example, if another boat didn't have to be started immediately, the

A letter Ed wrote in 1942 to the manager of North Pacific Cannery, confirming an order for five gillnetters. BILL PHILIPPSON COLLECTION

Mr. Harris,
    Manager , N.P.Cannery,
       Skeena River, B.C.

Dear Sir;
        I offer to build 5 gillnet boats and supply all labour and material necessary at a price of $ 630.00 each. ; demensions , material and net room, wheelhouse, and cabin arrangements to be the same as sample boat here, except the following alterations: the hull to made I4 ins. longer over stern post , cabin part of boat 3 ins higher.
        Net guard, rudder and steering outfit not included. Excise Tax if any, not included.

                                      Signed *Ed Wahl* .
                                          Box 942,
                                          Prince Rupert,B.C.

upper construction of a boat could occur on the building floor instead of in a stall or on the cradle.

Since the boats could be launched only on a high tide, they could remain inside the boat shop for up to a week; sometimes several boats were launched at the same time.

Preparation was the key to making this process work smoothly. All components were ready to go exactly when they were needed. This started with having the keel assembly for the next boat sitting on the side ready to be brought down to the building floor as soon as a spot opened up. The rest of the materials, including ribs and planks, were precut in an initial batch before construction started and then throughout the whole construction process the rate at which the lumber was cut matched the rate it was consumed.

Another major efficiency point of the assembly-line process was the use of moulds (or forms), wooden patterns or templates that were temporarily attached in specific locations along the entire keel to define the hull shape. Once the framing was completed, the moulds were removed and stacked just off to the side until the keel was laid for the next boat, when they would be pulled down to the floor again and attached to that keel to define its hull. The same moulds were used boat after boat, providing cookie-cutter construction, even though boat dimensions varied at the request of the customer.

"They weren't getting a heck of a lot for them little gill-netters from the canneries," Malcolm Elder explained, "so they were tossed up pretty fast. Sometimes they leaked a little bit, so you had to bring them back and we'd recork them a little. Sometimes they would be brought back in if we had to put more lumber into it. But if they couldn't have worked so fast, they wouldn't have been so successful!"

The *Laila II*: A Nod to the Japanese Boat Builders

The Olafsons were one of the first families in Osland, a small Icelandic settlement located on Smith Island at the mouth of the Skeena River. The father, Olafur or Oly, was a Skeena River fisherman who, along with Ed Wahl, began fishing on the river with a gas-powered boat while most fishermen were still using oar and sail. His first boat was the *Laila*, but he later had Ed build the *Laila II*, for which a design concept was borrowed from another boat-building family in the area, the Sakamotos.

After moving from Port Essington, the Sakamoto family had started boat building in Osland in the early 1930s in a converted airplane hangar purchased from Seal Cove. They were turning out cannery gillnet boats in high numbers at a time when Ed was mostly building trollers at Wahl Boatyard. Oly very much admired the Sakamoto design, especially the stern because it was rounder and fuller than the typical double-ender and provided more room for working and storing fish and more buoyancy in a following sea.

In early 1942, before the Sakamotos were sent to an internment camp in the Interior, they left their half-models with the Olafson family for safekeeping. "My dad showed Ed the model," said Carl, Oly's youngest son, "because he wanted the stern [on the *Laila II*] a little bit fuller so that, when he got into gillnetting, he could put a drum in there and he'd have room on both sides for fish pockets and that. He wanted a little bit of a bigger boat, too, than what the Japanese were making—just the ordinary

Oly Olafson aboard the Laila II *at Osland.*
CARL OLAFSON COLLECTION

The stern of the Full Moon.
RYAN WAHL COLLECTION

little double-ended gillnetters—so he asked ol' Ed Wahl to make it a little longer, a little wider and a little higher, which he, of course, could do."

When Ed built the boat during the winter of 1944, the fullness of the stern presented a planking challenge, but the new boat was ready early the following year and, when the *Laila II* hit the water, its unconventional stern became an instant centre of attention. Would it hold together? How would it perform? To the delight of everyone, especially Oly and Ed, the stern was a success, which is why it found its way into numerous future Wahl gillnetters and trollers, including the *Tracer*, the *Cobb* and the *Full Moon*.

"It was a dandy design," Carl said. "After that, all the company boats were designed after that model, including those at North Pacific and Canadian Fish. The trollers, they didn't need the real full stern like that because [the crew] just stood in the cockpit and pulled up their lines. But after that, the trollers wanted that stern, too, so they had more room to put their gear and had a little bit bigger cockpit to work with."

After being released from the internment camp, most members of the Sakamoto family didn't return to the West Coast and instead moved east to Toronto and Montreal. Many years later, as a self-rewarding act, Carl travelled across the country and returned the half-models to them. To him the Sakamotos were "good people and good shipwrights," a sentiment generally echoed by those who remember the great contributions to the commercial fishing industry made by the Japanese citizens of British Columbia.

Japanese Relocation

After 1942, production at the Wahl Boatyard was under even more pressure as a result of the removal of all Canadian citizens of Japanese descent from coastal areas. The Japanese bombing of Pearl Harbor on December 7, 1941, prompted the Canadian government to question the loyalty of persons of Japanese descent living in British Columbia, and in the early months of 1942 all Japanese on the West Coast were stripped of their rights, property and personal belongings and relocated to internment camps in the BC Interior. Over a thousand Japanese fishing boats were impounded and left sitting idle, leaving a huge void in the gillnet fleet. With all their Japanese boatbuilders gone, the North Coast canneries were forced to turn to the few non-Japanese boatyards in the area for all their new boats and it was the Wahl Boatyard that they came to rely on most.

This increased pressure meant another production expansion was necessary and a new building floor, to be used primarily for larger boats, was added on the opposite side of the shed. After this, construction of the cannery gillnetters occurred essentially wherever there was floor space, as well as on the two building floors, and because there was no time or room to spare, the pilothouse, the trunk cabin and the rest of the upper components were built inside the shop, in the stalls and on the cradle. The crew count increased to twenty-six (and peaked around thirty) and the shop operated six days a week, eleven to fourteen hours a day. According to Iver, in this heyday of the business as many as thirteen boats would be in the boat shop in various stages of construction or repair at one time, and with every last square foot of space used, construction almost spilled over to the outside. Because of the assembly-line process, upfront material preparation, sound management of a hard-working and dedicated crew, and improvements to the shed itself, a boat that used to take Ed and a couple of helping hands a whole winter to complete was now being built in a week—an incredible accomplishment for any boatyard on the coast. In 1943 and 1944, an average of one boat a week was launched out of the Wahl Boatyard.

According to Ernest, its single biggest order—for thirty-two boats—came in 1943 from Canadian Fishing Company. The following year the shop built forty-seven boats in ten months—forty gillnetters and seven 46-foot halibut boats—and in the year after that forty-three new boats were launched. On at least one occasion, a boat was built in five days.

Former worker Lenny Hadland described it as a "highball" shop. At the height of production, he witnessed canneries coming by to pick up as many as four new boats at once. "We were building two at once most of the time," Hadland said, "one on one side of the shed and another on the other side. There were also a couple of gillnetters planked up that were getting wheelhouses put on and a couple maybe getting the keel and the stems ready. I remember I was working with ol' man Ed Wahl and we were getting the stem- and sternposts and everything ready. As soon as we got that raised up, they started ribbing it. We'd rib a gillnet boat in the morning and start planking it in the afternoon. Iver—or whoever was looking after the ribs—would go to the steambox and grab a couple ribs, hand them to us and then get two more. By the time he came back, we were supposed to have [the first two] all nailed up. When we were ribbing, there was three of us, one inside the boat and one on each side. That was just when they were nailing the ribs right to the keel and after that there was just one of us on each side." Then he paused to explain, "The first ones, they were built more like a rowboat. They didn't have a keelson on them—they nailed the ribs right to the keel. Afterwards, they started putting in a keelson so if a keel got damaged they could drop it and they wouldn't have to tear the boat apart.

The halibut boat Connie-Jean.
ED AND DIANE WAHL COLLECTION

When I started planking, there were two of us on one side and two on the other. It took about a day and a half to plank it."

Vidar Sandhals remembers Henry and others fighting to get large cedar "crooks" through the band saw. "You know the shape of a bowstem, how it sweeps upward? We used to go up the Ecstall River and the Skeena and locate these trees because we knew where the yellow

cedars grew out of the riverbanks. The tree grows out of the bank and then, of course, it naturally turns and grows upward, and the bowstems were made from these yellow cedar crooks. In those days we used to shape them by manhandling them through a band saw. They would get a couple of guys steering this thing into the band saw— they were quite large, maybe six or eight feet long—and we were trying to hold them up to get the right angle. And then the band saw blade would come off the guide because they couldn't keep the thing steady. Henry would be in on that. He was small but strong and wiry. Lots of guts. After, Henry looked like he'd climbed a barbed wire fence. Nowadays, they fabricate [the bowstems] out of timbers and bolts."

The gillnetters constructed on the building floor were launched as complete boats by placing them on piping and then pushing them until they came to the end of the floor. A rope tied to the bow prevented them from getting away. Those built on the higher portions of the boat shop were launched by pushing them along a greased floor—if they were light enough. Otherwise they were first placed on rollers. They were then pushed out one of the side doors. "Wherever there was a door, we shoved 'em out!" Roald, Ed's son, said.

On one exciting evening in 1947, the halibut boat *Connie-Jean* and five gillnetters were launched at once. Two of the gillnetters capsized when they hit the water. "The tide had dropped so much by the time we got them to the end of the floor that there wasn't much water there, so they just fell off the end and capsized," Iver said. "No ballast, light as a feather. But nothing was hurt. They looked so funny with their keels up in the air. We got them over by the floor and picked them up by the wheelhouse and bailed them out. And away they went."

One of the keys to Ed Wahl's success was the kind treatment he showed his neighbours, crew and customers. Standing just five feet eight inches, he was a short but formidable presence and, to the younger family members, he was so much bigger than life that they saw him as

Melvin Closter in 2001 with his accordion, his most prized possession. DIANE WHEELER COLLECTION

Melvin Closter was typical of the young men who came to work at the Wahl Boatyard in those years. At twenty-four he had left the family farm in Weldon, Saskatchewan, in 1939, and headed for Oona River where his relative, Julius Hadland, had a sawmill. After one winter working there, he got a job at the Prince Rupert Drydock and Shipyard and for the next three years worked on the construction of the large steel freighters needed for the war effort. Then in 1944, with his new wife Sadie, Melvin moved to Dodge Cove. "I got the job [at the Wahl Boatyard] as I had a cousin living in Dodge Cove and he knew the Wahls. He mentioned that I should move there, so I did and was hired on," Melvin said. "I started out as a helper, then after getting acquainted with the work, I ended up being able to do most of the jobs that we were given to do—putting on planking, doing the decking, working on the bulwarks, rubbing the guardrails with gumwood, drum stands, doors, puttying seams, trunk cabinets and more."

Melvin started at the Wahl Boatyard at a time when it was steadily pumping out gillnet boats for the canneries, but throughout the next couple of decades, he saw first-hand the transition from mass gillnet boat production to the production of "bigger and better" boats for other fisheries.

quite intimidating. But among his peers and crew and throughout the fishing community he was known and respected as a kind, gentle man who went about his work in a stalwart and steady fashion.

He inspired immense loyalty in his workers even though he pushed them to their limits when it came to getting boats out on time. And he was death on unions. When it was suggested that he unionize his shops, Iver recalled that it was a case of "Holy crap, no damn way! Start talking unions with Dad was the only way you could get him mad. The union rep came over I don't know how many times to the Wahl Boatyards to talk about starting a union. 'Like hell,' Dad said, 'there'll be a union around here.' Dad never swore, you know, except that time. My crew, he says, are pleased where they are and I'll beat these bunch of so-and-so's any old time when it comes to the wages.' And it was true because he did."

"Oh, Ed was a real nice guy," recalled Vidar Sandhals. "So easygoing, you know. I never heard him raise his voice I don't think ever. He didn't need to crack the whip." Art Stace-Smith, who was twenty years old and as green as they come when he started working for Ed in 1957, said, "I went over to Digby and asked your great-granddad Ed Wahl for a job. He hired me right on the spot. The Wahls were very well known for their boat-building skills, but I had never met them before that day. I worked for them for three or four winters … The second time I asked him for a job—I was married by then—Ed says, 'You can start tomorrow or right now if you want to.' He kinda thought I might have been a bit short on cash and quite honestly I was. 'I'll pay you right now if you want.' He was that kind of a guy. He was a great guy, I'm telling you. He had excellent character and was very kind to the fishing fleet. You had to like him … I worked on the building of one of the bigger additions to the boat shop and a dock for loading freight and supplies for the shop. Ed was there, working right along with two or three of us. We set the pilings, did the structure, the roof and the whole thing. It took about a month to build. Sometimes if the tide was low in the evenings we had to work late to set pilings and at these times all the Wahl brothers worked right alongside us—as well as building boats during the day."

"Ed, he was a real honest person," said former employee Harold Johnson. "He didn't try to gyp anybody. He was such a solid, steady guy." When it came to sealing a deal to build a boat, his handshake was worth as much, if not more, than his signature on the contract. His former accountant and bookkeeper, Odd Eidsvik, told a story that underlined this fact. "My dad had the boat *Keno No. 2* built by Ed Wahl in 1945. After I started doing the books over there in the later part of the 1950s, a fellow came in one day and said he would like Ed to build a boat like the *Keno 2* for him but a couple of feet longer. I was there doing the books as the two of them were talking. This man wondered how much it would cost and what kind of engine it was going to have and all the rest of it. Ed said, 'You come back tomorrow.' So he came back the next day and I had happened to be back there, too—I would take the boat over from the Co-op plant every day when the guys went to work. Ed said, 'Yeah, I can do it for you. It'll be a little bit longer than Eidsvik's boat so it's going to be a little more money. I figure it's going to cost about $16,500. It'll have a Chrysler engine but it's not one of the big ones—it's an in-between one. We'll finish the inside for you to your specifications but we won't put any fishing gear on it or anything else. Like, you know, no pots and pans.' And the guy says, '$16,500 sounds like a fair price.' And then Ed said, 'And before we start I need

Box 942,
Prince Rupert, B.C.
Dec. 16th. 1942.

National War Services
MA-5748
4541

Mr. Harris,
    Manager, North Pacific Cannery,
        Vancouver, B.C.

Dear Mr. Harris:
            I would appreciate it very much if you
would be kind enough to personally call on the Hon.
Judge Manson, National War Service Division "K",
Yorkshire Bldg. and ask for postponement from military
service, for Henry E. Wahl (No. K51245).
            I have written to the National War
Service Division "K", asking for a postponement and the
letter was endorsed by Mr. Jarvis McLeod, of Prince
Rupert, but I thought it would be better if you would
see Judge Manson and explain the situation to him.
Henry has been working in the boatshop for five years
and at the present time it is impossible to hire a
skilled man to take his place.

                    Yours truly, *Ed Wahl*

A letter Ed wrote to the North Pacific Cannery.
BILL PHILIPPSON COLLECTION

$5,000, when we get three-quarters of the way along, I'd
like another $5,000 and when we launch her for you, I'd
like the rest of the money.' They shook hands and he built
the boat. That's the way it worked."

"I can guarantee he lived up to his side of the deal,"
said Art Stace-Smith. "When the customer crapped on
Ed, I'm sure he just said he's the loser and I'll just keep
building."

January 7 1943

National War Service Commission.K.
Yorkshire Building.
Vancouver.B.C.

Dear Sirs:-

   re Application for Postponement-Henry E.Wahl No.K51245

        I have to-day forwarded to the above the necessary
forms for this man and his father,for whom he is working,to
complete same.
        The father.Ed Wahl.operates a boat-building and
repair shop at Dodge Cove in Rupert Harbor. They have built
boats for us in the past and we are relying on them to build
ten gill-net boats for us this Spring . These boats are badly
needed to maintain our fishing fleet as we made no replacements
last year due to the evacuation of the Japanese on whom we
principally relied for the building of gill-net boats.
        Henry Wahl is his father's right-hand man and most
skilful assistant and the output of the boatshop will be badly
crippled if deprived of his services.
                        Yours truly:-

A letter from the North Pacific Cannery to the National War Service Commission.
BILL PHILIPPSON COLLECTION

Wartime Service

Ed's three oldest boys, Henry, Iver and Ernest, were all
called up for war service. This was the last thing Ed wanted
to happen. Aside from living with the worry that his boys
would be injured or never return, he knew that he simply
could not run the business with all three of them gone.
Being the eldest, Henry was the most likely one to be
required to serve, but he was also the most vital son to
the business. Fortunately, Ed had the canneries on his side

because they understood what losing Henry would mean to them. The North Pacific Cannery, for one, showed its support by sending a letter to the National War Service Commission, expressing concern over Henry's potential departure.

The petitions were successful and Henry's war service was waived, but attention then shifted to Ed's next two sons. A visit by an army general to the shop forced Ed to make a swift decision on who would go. "Take the youngest one," he said. Ernest then packed his bags and went off to serve in the war. His enlistment was short-lived, however. According to my grandfather, Ernest served in the army in eastern Canada and then decided to volunteer to fight in the Pacific. He was just about to depart when the conflict there ended. A postwar physical examination, however, showed that he had contracted tuberculosis and he was admitted to Shaughnessy Hospital in Vancouver. "I was only nineteen years old when I went in there [the hospital]," Ernest said. "They take an X-ray when you go [into the army] and then they take one when they discharge you. They saw a little spot and they just took out one lobe [of a lung] to get rid of it. I didn't have much." During the next year and a half of strict bedrest, he turned this misfortune into something positive by studying naval architecture and was soon creating blueprints for boats that fell into the steamboat classification. "We got him to make the models," Iver said. "Dad and Henry took all the measurements and then gave [them] to Ernest and he drew it all up on paper. He was the only one that could do it. He was the one that, you know, did the blueprint work for us whenever we had to do that, which wasn't very often because everybody liked the models."

CHAPTER FOUR

TROLLERS AND SAWDUST

T he end of World War II caused a major population drop in Prince Rupert and activity along
the waterfront there declined significantly. The
town's prosperity continued, however, and commercial
boat building remained strong. In the early postwar years,
Prince Rupert was recognized as one of the main boat-
building centres in the province. The continued strong
demand for Wahl boats reflected this.

Between 1946 and 1949 Wahl Boatyard built at least
two 46-foot packers—the *Island Point* in 1946 for the
Canadian Fishing Company for $5,500 and one for the
North Pacific Cannery in 1949 that cost them $7,185.
The boatyard also supplied gillnet boats to BC Packers,
the Canadian Fishing Company Ltd., the Cassiar Packing
Company, the North Pacific Cannery, the Carlisle Cannery
and Atlin Fisheries Ltd. (a subsidiary of Canadian Fishing
Company). Their standard gillnetter remained 32 feet
long but the average price over this time span rose from
$1,100 to $1,800.

What is more interesting about this four-year period
is the fluctuation in the number of orders Wahl Boatyard
received for gillnetters. In 1946 Ed and his sons built about
the same number as they had the year before—thirty-five
gillnetters—plus two trollers, one halibut boat, one packer
and a boat of an unspecified type for Captain J. Strand. But

The north end of Dodge Cove viewed from "CBC Hill," so named for the Canadian Broadcasting Corporation repeater station atop it. The Wahl Boatyard is in the upper left corner and the Wahl sawmill is in the upper right corner. Below is the CBC repeater station and the residence of the station caretaker that were erected in the early 1940s. Also on the hill was a Department of Transport weather and wireless station built in the early 1900s.
ROALD AND VIOLET WAHL COLLECTION

according to 1947 financial records, the number of gillnet boats produced at the family boatyard in that year was just seventeen, half the number produced in 1946. The following year, the number fell by half again. The setback turned out to be a temporary one and in 1949 production was on the rise again. The two-year decline in production was actually a blessing because it gave the Wahls a chance finally to catch their collective breath after the tumultuous years since the start of the war. "We'd been going full bore for about ten years," Iver said. "We built anywhere from thirty-six to forty [gillnet boats] every year and that was just for the one cannery. We built them for every cannery on the coast right down to Vancouver and up in Alaska and down in America. We were going twelve and four-teen hours a day and damn near running double shift. But

APRIL 10	1 gill-net hull Cassiar Packing Co. No. 1.	1450.00	1450.00
28	1 gill-net hull Cassiar Packing Co. No. 2.	1450.00	1450.00
29	"Lilimak II" packer. J. J. Maki	15.00	15.00
10	1 gill net hull. Canadian Fishing Co.	1175.00	1175.00
25	"Sandy S" salmon troller Capt. A. Sandhals.	2800.00	2800.00
19	"P. Doreen" - halibut vessel. Capt. L. Sandvar.	1267.65	1267.65
30	"Connie Jean" halibut vessel Capt. J. Lundstrom	5500.00	5500.00

A page from the boatyard's general ledger for March and April 1947.
ED AND DIANE WAHL COLLECTION

then it got so we couldn't take it anymore and we just cut her down." Ed took the opportunity to return the shop to pre-war work hours and he cut back to just thirteen men at the boatyard, not including his six sons.

In this return to normalcy, the Wahls had time to implement another major improvement to the boatyard. Before 1948/1949 fuel for the boatyard's gas engines, especially those that powered the band saws and the planer, had been a significant portion of the monthly operating costs, but the new shop was wired for electricity, substantially reducing costs. A Caterpillar generator was brought in to supply the power, electric motors replaced the gas engines on the machinery and new light fixtures were installed. At the same time the Wahl homes were also wired for lights, replacing the kerosene lamps used previously. However, when Ed realized that the Caterpillar engine provided too much power for just running the lights at the Wahl homes at night, he brought in a small-output Lidster diesel "light plant," and the Caterpillar was shut down each day after the boatyard's working hours.

During those near double-shift years the family's personal circumstances had changed. Ed had married again in 1942. Mary Jean Mathers had come from Sandspit on Moresby Island to be the Dodge Cove schoolteacher. Together Ed and Mary had two children—Helen and John—and they built a new house together on a plot of land adjacent to the boatyard. Sadly, Mary died of cancer of the liver in October 1948.

Ed's eldest son, Henry, had married Violet Wick in July 1946 and Iver served as Henry's best man. On March 2 of that year, twenty-one-year-old Iver had met his soulmate, Mary Skog, while at a birthday party in Prince Rupert. "We all had a good time [at the party]," Mary recalled, "and then in the wee hours of the morning we decided

Henry and his wife, Violet, on their wedding day in 1946. Iver was Henry's best man. ROALD AND VIOLET WAHL COLLECTION

to go on a fishing trip with your grandfather's brother Henry. So we all headed over to Dodge Cove. It was my first trip there. It was all dark, not a single light was on over there. The boys picked up their gumboots and then off we went to do some fishing. All we had to eat aboard was fruitcake and canned vegetable soup. It was March so the weather was unpredictable. We got out there and

Iver and Mary on their wedding day and many years later.
MARY WAHL COLLECTION

a storm brews up. The men had quite a time with the oil barrels on the deck, trying to take care of them, otherwise they would have tipped. When we started heading back to town again, I was up in the wheelhouse and your grandfather's brother yells, 'Look back and you won't get seasick!' I was never so happy to see the likes of Prince Rupert."

That summer Iver and Mary dated frequently, going to shows and dances, including those sponsored by the Sons of Norway. They married on October 12 of that same year and moved in with Henry and Violet. About a year later Henry and Violet built a new house across the road, and Iver and Mary set out to build a house next door to them. At the same time they commissioned a sawmill worker to build them a small "maiden house" right behind their house that was being built. "It was our first home. It only had two rooms—a kitchen and a bedroom," Mary said. "We didn't even have a bathroom but we had an outhouse. Our first fridge was a cooler out on the porch. I remember I put a lemon pie out there to cool and a squirrel came and started eating it." They moved into their new house before it was completely finished.

"When Mary and I first married," said Iver, "I left in the morning and ran home for fifteen or twenty minutes for lunch and then I ran again. Supper was the same and then after supper I never got home until eleven or twelve o'clock every night!" And Mary agreed that "he was right there, you know. He'd come home for lunch and supper, but they were so busy they had to go back and work till maybe eleven o'clock at night. They did this when they were in a rush to get a boat ready to send to the cannery." Iver and Mary had two sons—Gary (my father) in 1947 and Larry ten years later.

The Wahl Sawmill

In the early years of the Wahl Boatyard, maintaining a steady supply of lumber hadn't been a problem for Ed. With only half a dozen boats a year coming out of the shed, his needs were easily met by local mills, including John Group's mill at Oona River, the Georgetown Mill near Port Simpson and Brown's Mill just below Port Essington.

Krist Iverson also supplied lumber to the Wahl Boatyard, travelling the twenty-five miles from his mill at Oona River to Dodge Cove in his fishing boat to deliver the order. His son Norman recalled that "Ed and my dad were great friends. The old man made an agreement with Ed that he would take all [the lumber my dad] could produce. [My father] used to go out and do a bit of logging and then he would have the stuff sawed up. He towed the lumber in rafts right up to the shed at Dodge Cove. From there they put the lumber right on the carriage and then took it up into the shed."

After 1939, however, the war effort put a serious strain on Canada's forest industry and mill operations. With physically fit men taken out of the forest to serve in the forces, there was a shortage of labour to fell the trees and mill the wood. Adding to the problem was the increased demand for Canadian timber from other countries, especially the United States. Priority for the remaining timber went to any industry that was directly supporting the war effort; whatever was left was spread among the many industries that used wood in some fashion. All these factors resulted in a demand that far exceeded supply. In Prince Rupert the sawmills were under even more pressure because of the local increase in troops and the resulting building boom and, when boat production also surged during the

The Miss Teresa, *the cruiser Iver and Mary built in the evenings and on week-ends. It was powered by a 220-hp Crusader V8 marine gas engine. "My pride and joy," said Iver. "That was the day we launched it. Larry and your dad were aboard, and they were going to take her out for a trial run. They were playing around with it for a half a day."* MELAINE FILLION COLLECTION

war years, the mills couldn't keep up.

This lumber supply crisis continued even after the war's end and Ed was finally forced to consider alternative sources. In 1946 he leased six acres in a bay to the north of the boatyard and erected his own two-storey sawmill. He purchased a saw from Vancouver and a 110 International

The Wahl Boatyard in the late 1940s or early 1950s. Gillnet boats were launched off the main building floor out of the open doors on the left (above the boat in the water). In the centre on the cradle is Island Queen I. *To the right of the main building is the separate stall that "had just the bare necessities—a plank walk-around so you could get onto the boat. That was about it. At high water it would float," said former employee Vidar Sandhals.*

ANTON RAMFJORD JR. COLLECTION

J ulius Hadland had established the well-known sawmill at Oona River in 1921. An immigrant from Norway around 1902, he had homesteaded in Saskatchewan, run a flour mill there and fished out of Prince Rupert before settling at Oona River with his family. By 1936 he had moved to Digby Island where he established Dodge Cove's first sawmill on Tobey Point. This mill was one of many in the area supplying lumber to the Canadian and US armed forces during World War II, some of it being used in the construction of barracks.

diesel engine from Winnipeg to run it. He bought a 110 Chrysler Industrial engine to run a planer and installed an edger alongside it. At start-up he had enough logs on hand to provide half a million board feet of lumber; another hundred thousand board feet were stored right outside in the bay and an additional four hundred thousand stored elsewhere, including a substantial amount just around the corner in Marine Bay. The main log suppliers were three handloggers who cut in areas close to the ocean and then towed the logs into the bay in front of the mill. Handloggers supplied most or all of the sawmills in the area, though the Wahl mill also received logs from beachcombers.

By the fall the sawmill was in full operation, producing an average of eight thousand board feet of planed lumber daily and at times producing as much as twelve thousand. At the start Ed took on the job of manager and hired a man to run the saw. Four years later twenty-year-old Roald left the boatyard to work in the mill full-time and for the next twelve years he served as foreman and bookkeeper and as a sawyer whenever needed. When he left the mill to work in the boatyard again, the last main sawyer was Walter Davis, who served the longest of

The Wahl sawmill with the Wahl Boatyard visible farther down the shoreline.
RYAN WAHL COLLECTION

all the hired sawyers. "We did the sawing, Walter and I," Roald said. "We were together the whole time and I was kind of the foreman of the mill. I looked after most of it, including the bookkeeping. I got the orders from my dad who sawed a bit, too." When lumber was needed in the boatyard, the company workboat scurried over to the sawmill and docked at its loading platform. Lumber was pulled out of the drying shed and stacked onto the deck of the workboat, which then had a short return journey to the boatyard to make the delivery. "That's how we ran things," said Roald. "There was only four or five of us working there, but later there was quite a few more."

Art Stace-Smith, who "started out at the sawmill, first with Walter Davis as sawyer and then with Roald Wahl as sawyer," remembered "cutting boat lumber, edge-grain planking and other boat materials—hard work but good for you." As well as supplying the boatyard, the Wahl sawmill also filled orders for both lumber and logs for external customers. In the early postwar years, the mill supplied the US army, which still occupied Port Edward. During this period twelve men were employed in the mill and, according to Roald, it ran "practically all day and night." Steady orders came in from independent fishermen and local canneries that needed lumber for repairing their fishing boats. Hemlock and spruce were cut and planed for local construction. (Although neither of these trees make good boat planking, they are perfectly suitable for shiplap—an inexpensive tongue-and-groove board used primarily as siding.) The mill also cut lumber for waterfront projects such as dock building. The largest customers of the Wahl sawmill included the local tugboat company Armour Salvage, the Department of Fisheries, the Prince Rupert Drydock and Shipyard and Columbia Cellulose, which probably used the Wahl lumber for the construction of the pulp mill at Port Edward.

Having his own mill meant Ed had control over product quality from start to finish. For the boatyard the sawmill cut edge-grain softwood, primarily western redcedar and secondarily yellow cedar and spruce. Redcedar was used for the hull planking of the gillnetters, yellow cedar for deck beams and components of the backbone including the horn timber and sternpost, and spruce for the booms, masts and penboards. Some hemlock was cut for the boat-yard as well, but it was used only for the keelson of the gillnetters when fir couldn't be delivered in time for that purpose. Fir was also used for deck planking and for the keel and the hull planking on the larger boats. Douglas fir is not indigenous to the North Coast, although some fir logs did occasionally drift north and beachcombers would collect them and sell them to the mill. Most of the necessary fir was purchased from the well-known Vancouver lumberyard J. Fyfe Smith Co. Ltd. and shipped north by barge. This lumberyard also supplied the hardwoods—oak and gumwood—needed for critical internal and outside components where strength and resistance to friction were essential. Oak was used for the ribs that made up the framing and gumwood went into the caps, guardrails and

The Dual *after it was converted into a yacht. "It was named* Dual *because it was a dual-purpose boat: a troller and a gillnetter," said previous owner Currie Ellis. He adds: "I've gone back and forth in it to Alaska a couple of times and to fancy resorts all over and the boat has always been very well received. You can park it next to all them million-dollar fibreglass yachts and it's the one that gets the attention."* CURRIE ELLIS COLLECTION

false keels (the protective layer for the keel).

Fyfe Smith's mill had specialized in cutting hardwoods since the early 1900s and Wahl Boatyard had established a strong professional relationship with the mill that lasted for decades. Ed rarely had issues with orders from Smith, but according to Malcolm Elder, a former Wahl Boatyard employee, the odd bad shipment was received. One was a batch of two-and-a-half- or three-inch heavy decking that was shipped frozen. When it arrived, the ice had to be pounded off before it could be put through the planer, but the wood had absorbed so much moisture that, when it dried, the entire deck of a boat on which it had been used had to be recaulked.

The Rise of the Trollers

While the production of gillnetters had begun to wane in the early postwar years, trollers had become more and more important in the fishing industry, and in Prince Rupert troller production rose to a new level. The Wahl troller was in especially high demand.

Trolling, which had begun in BC waters during World War I, appealed to fishermen because it allowed economic independence. Unlike gillnet fishermen, trollers weren't indentured to the canneries and were free to explore other markets to get the best possible price for their catch. The other positive aspect was the relatively low cost of getting into the fishery. In gillnetting there was a substantial initial cost in purchasing a net and then maintaining it thereafter. Hooking a net on a reef or having a boat run over the net meant hundreds of dollars in repair bills or the purchase of a new net. In trolling, however, the capital investment in lines, hooks, lures and other gear was far less. According to Roald, trolling had been "popular all the time" since

A young Bobby installing the front decking of an unknown boat. On the assembly line, Bobby led the way on the wheelhouses and trunk cabins.
ERNEST AND KAY WAHL COLLECTION

his dad had started building in Dodge Cove, and the boat-yard would continue to produce these boats throughout the 1950s. Typically Wahl trollers ranged between 36 feet and 42 feet, though some were built larger. For Roald, it was the trollers and other independent fishermen who made the work especially rewarding. "It would not have been much of a boatyard without their business," he said. Halibut boats, cabin cruisers and a dory rounded out the other boat types built for private buyers between 1946 and 1949.

The Banner No. 2. *Both the* Connie-Jean *and* Banner No. 2 *had a fantail stern, which was standard on Wahl halibut boats and trollers in the 1940s. It is also the type of stern typically found on yachts and sailboats.*

JACK PRINCE COLLECTION

idar Sandhals: "Ed built a lot of boats for individuals. In fact, he built one for my brother, Arvid—a 33-foot troller called the *Osprey*. I went trolling with him on it. We had a wash basin in it that came out of one of the Skeena River boats that sat on the beach in Port Essington. There were three river boats sitting there rotting away. The wash basin came from SS *Inlander* that used to run up to Hazelton. Later [in 1947] Arvid got a second boat by Ed. It was *Sandy S*, a 38-footer."

The Island Queen

In 1948 Ed and his sons Henry, Iver and Ernest went into partnership to build the 50-foot longliner *Island Queen I* for themselves. It was powered by an 80-hp Caterpillar engine. For the first few years Henry ran it as a halibut boat then left it to his father and brothers in order to build his own boat. A couple of years later Nels Antonsen was skippering the boat but by 1954 the skipper was Otto Olsen (Ed's brother-in-law) and Iver was working as his deckhand. One summer Iver was also part of a five-man crew that fished with this boat in Alaska. "We had just a compass and a chart," said Iver. "No radar or nothing else. It sure was some nerve-racking. Well, lots of times we just anchored up. I wouldn't take a chance because we didn't even have insurance on the boat. I wanted to insure it but Dad said it cost too much." After that Iver served as captain of the boat for one season when he packed salmon for the North Pacific Cannery.

Eventually Ernest bought his father's and brothers' shares in the *Island Queen I* and rigged it for the seine fishery, although he had no intention of running it himself. "I took it across the harbour to Rupert—that's the closest I ever come to running it," he said. Instead, Harry Olsen

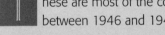

These are most of the commercial fishing boats Wahl Boatyard built for private buyers between 1946 and 1949:

- *Pauline V* (1946) – 46-foot halibut boat
- *Dual* (1946) – 41-foot troller
- *Valiant* (1946) – 40-foot troller
- *Lone Rock* (1947) – 36-foot troller
- *Salal* (1947) – troller
- *Sandy S* (1947) – 38-foot troller
- *Connie-Jean* (1947) – halibut boat
- *Hike* (1947) – 47-foot troller
- *Spray No. 1* (1948) – 40-foot troller
- *Bev-Marie* (1948) – 38-foot troller
- *North Pacific* (1948) – 48-foot troller
- *Ramsay Isle* (1948) – 42-foot troller
- *Island Queen I* (1948) – 50-foot halibut boat
- Unnamed – 33-foot gillnet boat built for a Bella Coola customer
- *Vance* (1949) – 46-foot troller
- *Banner No. 2* (1949) – 46-foot troller
- *Advise* (1949) – 45-foot halibut boat
- *Comfort II* (1949) – 42-foot troller

The Island Queen I *when owned by Harry Olsen, rigged for the halibut fishery and sporting a dodger. On board is the Olsen family. The next owner of the boat rolled it over in deep water in Granville Channel.* KEN OLSEN COLLECTION

(cousin to the Wahl brothers) skippered it for him and eventually bought the boat. Harry fished halibut with a full crew and, according to his son Ken, put the boat to its limits by offshore fishing in areas of the Gulf of Alaska where winds reach one hundred knots. "My dad sure put that boat through its paces," he said. "He was in a hurricane once. After it hit about seventy-five knots, he said

The Island Queen I *in the 1950s at the Dodge Cove wharf. Iver was captain at the time. "We just got home [from salmon packing] and were getting ready to clean her up and throw her on the carriage for a paint job," Ernest said.*
MARY WAHL COLLECTION

the wind started to take the tops off the waves. The *Island Queen* got smashed up pretty good that time—the dodger smashed off, the cabin was pushed back, the mast was flopping back and forth, planking sprung off the bulwarks and the force of the waves bent the anchor winch. The waves also knocked out the windows and the cabin started filling up with water, and soon Dad was up to his waist in it. Everybody kind of thought they were drowning until the water starting running off into the engine room and fo'c'sle and then onto the deck. Once the water ran off, they got the boat swung around so the stern was in the weather. They ripped the cupboard doors off and patched up the front of the wheelhouse. The *Island Queen* was looking pretty sad when it come into Rupert Harbour."

After ten years of solid production with it, Harry sold the boat and got out of the halibut fishery altogether. "He was getting tired of digging crews out of beer parlours," his son said. "If I'd wanted the *Island Queen*, he would have saved it for me but I was too young. I didn't know what I wanted to do." Much later Harry Olsen asked Ernest to build him a smaller boat than the *Island Queen*, one he could manage on his own with a single deckhand. By then Ernest was producing boats in Salmon Arm, and he built the 41-foot troller *Sandy Point* there for Harry and trucked it down to the Fraser River.

The *Island Queen* was the first and the last boat built by the family for the family. Ed's sons, of course, built many fishing boats for themselves.

The 1950s

In the boatyards of the 1950s, boat designs were undergoing evolutionary change from bow to stern and in large part the improvements were made possible by advancements in the engine room. As the horsepower of the modern marine diesel engine increased, the constraints on boat construction decreased, allowing shipwrights and naval architects more flexibility and creativity in their designs. For Ed Wahl this meant that his ideas about aesthetic design could begin to mature. His straight lines became curved, his sharp corners became rounded and the Wahl boats that finally emerged in the late 1950s had all the eye-pleasing characteristics that would make them so recognizable along the entire BC coast.

The steady increase in horsepower meant that boat construction could be less concerned with trimming width and weight to achieve the standard cruising speed. In the midsection widening the beams became the preferred alternative to the traditional boat design. First, such widening increased the capacity of the fish hold and the larger the hold volume the longer the fishermen could stay out on the fishing grounds. Second, it increased the working space on deck. Third, it lowered the centre of gravity and thus improved stability. Although it is true that the broader the beam the higher the resistance, any decrease in speed caused by the new designs was made up for by ample engine horsepower.

In the aft section widening the beams permitted the option of installing a transom (or square) stern. This became a popular choice because it provided high buoyancy and ample working space for handling the nets, gear and fish. A transom stern was especially helpful in the gillnet boats because it prevented the stern from squatting—or lowering—at high speeds. In trollers, the transom stern was practically a necessity to handle the larger beams and increasingly powerful marine engines that were being installed. By the end of the 1950s, the transom stern had surpassed the traditional double-ender stern in popularity,

although over the next decade a few Wahl boats were still built with the traditional stern when the buyers asked for it.

The wheelhouse greatly benefited from widening the hull as well. When the hull width was increased, naturally the width of the wheelhouse could be increased, too. This meant that the galley could be brought up from the fo'c'sle, allowing fishermen to make dinner without having to take a peek upstairs periodically to check on the boat's operation. This "galley-on-deck" style wheelhouse, already commonplace on larger boats, gained popularity in trollers during the 1950s and within the decade became a standard in wheelhouse design. The additional space also led to a tendency to bring in all the creature comforts of home to make the long trips and harbour days on the anchor more enjoyable.

The classic West Coast troller for which the Wahls became so well known emerged from these improvements in boat design. One of defining characteristics of the Wahl troller was the stave stern, which is flat like a transom but has rounded corners and is heavily "timbered" to provide a very sturdy assembly. In a stave stern—also known as a timber-and-picket stern—the stave or picket is the lower section made up of slightly off-vertical pieces and the timbered portion is the upper section made up of timbers laid horizontally on each other. Separating the two sections is the guard that runs almost the entire length of the boat.

Although the general trend was toward increased production of trollers, near the end of the 1950s production of gillnet boats continued to be strong at the Wahl

Opposite: *A transom stern Wahl gillnet boat newly delivered to North Pacific Cannery.* COURTESY OF NORTH PACIFIC PAPERS, NORTH PACIFIC CANNERY NHS, PORT EDWARD, BC

The choice of stern for the Wahl troller was the stave stern. It was flat like a transom but had rounded corners and was heavily timbered to provide a very sturdy assembly. In a stave stern (also know as a timber-and-picket stern) the stave or picket is the lower section that is made up of slightly off-vertical pieces and the timbered portion is the upper section made up of timbers laid horizontally on each other. Separating the two sections is the guard that runs almost the entire length of the boat. The stave stern, as shown here on the San Mateo was one of the defining characteristics of the Wahl troller.

RYAN WAHL COLLECTION

M alcolm Elder: "The Wahls could build a better boat for the dollar than anybody else—and you can say that with confidence." He had served in the army during World War II, fished for a few years and then spent a few more years as a logger before Ed Wahl hired him. "I had a logging accident and figured I wouldn't be able to do the woods anymore because I couldn't flex my foot. That's how I got into the Wahl's boatyard. It turned out I probably could have gone on logging because I got around quite well with it, but anyway I started working in the shed." Malcolm's logging experience landed him the role of "spar man," making the booms and the masts. He worked for the Wahls for 12 years, and his initial orientation of boatyard operations would have included an overview of the general work philosophy: each member of the crew would be exposed to every aspect of boat building so that on a moment's notice anyone could jump out of one area and into another. Even the specialists, such as the plankers, who mostly planked all day, still had to be able to do the other jobs. "We saw everything around. There are a lot of jobs you can do in a shop like that—you got the planers, the band saws and the other tools to keep sharp. Somebody has got to do it. I didn't go there to be a carpenter and I stayed away from carpentry as much as I could, but every once in a while I'd get pushed into it and get caught on that job all day."

Boatyard. Just over a decade had passed since the end of World War II and many of the gillnetters built during the war had reached the end of their life cycle and had to be replaced. As well, a good portion of them were simply too small to be effective in the fishery any longer. This prompted the canneries to go shopping again on a larger scale. The following letter written in 1957 by Ole

The *San Mateo:* From Highline Troller to Coastal Cruiser

From gillnetter to troller to yacht, the *San Mateo* has worn many faces during her fifty years of existence. On October 30, 1956, Ed Wahl began work on this 40-foot by 12-foot by 6-foot-10-inch boat for Dave Moore. The price was $8,250. According to Dave's son, Bruce, the *San Mateo*—along with her sister ships, the *Fairview II* and the *Silver Mist*—was initially designed as a deep-sea gillnetter, but due to a change in government regulations around deep-sea gillnetting, the boat became a troller. The trio was launched in early 1957 and later that year the *San Mateo* and the *Fairview II* were pictured with two other boats in *Western Fisheries* magazine as "highline trollers."

After going solo on his inaugural trip, Dave hauled Bruce out of school to fish with him the rest of that season and Bruce then deckhanded on the boat for a few more years. Dave's homestead on the fishing grounds was Hecate Strait, an area with which he was already familiar. "He dragged there for twenty or thirty years," Bruce said. "He knew Hecate Strait, the Horseshoe and the rest of those places. We didn't have radar. You'd look for a mountain—and hope to God you could see it—and go by your depth. The old man always fished thirty-three to thirty-five fathoms and that's how I navigated." The *San Mateo* had just an Ekolite recorder and flasher, charts and a compass.

With sheer determination—and perhaps a touch of stubbornness—Dave Moore took his boat into the worst of conditions while the bulk of the fleet was safely anchored in a sheltered harbour.

"We've been in some strong winds, the ol' man and me," Bruce said. "Once we were fishing in thirty-five- and forty-knot winds off Banks Island. I said to him, 'What the — are we doing out here? The boat is moving up and down so much the fish can't bite the — hooks. All you're doing is burning fuel and you're not going to hook anything!' Salmon ain't going to bite a hook jumping up and down ten or twelve feet. He finally realized it was time to go in. There were forty trollers tied up in the harbour and we were the last boat in. I think we had twenty coho that day and we used to get two or three hundred."

In the late 1990s when Bent Jespersen of Jespersen Boat Builders Ltd. of Sidney, British Columbia, and his son Eric were looking for the perfect ex-fishing boat to convert to a family cruiser, they had many fishing boats that were no longer in the fleet from which to choose, but one boat stood out from the rest. They already knew of the *San Mateo* by reputation as a good sea boat and knew that it was well kept by the original and current owners, so when the boat became available, they immediately bought it and started planning the conversion. "The *San Mateo* was in good shape when we bought her, thanks to a large refit in the seventies," Eric said. "David Moore, the original owner, sold her to Jim Roberts of Sidney. We bought her from Jim."

The San Mateo, *a classic 1950s Wahl troller, on her launch day.*
COURTESY OF THE WRATHALL COLLECTION, PRINCE RUPERT CITY & REGIONAL ARCHIVES AND MUSEUM OF NORTHERN BC

The conversion started in the spring of 2000. In most conversions the wheelhouse is extended to provide additional accommodations, but in this case the fish hold was converted into a low-profile aft cabin. In this way, the deck beams and the classic West Coast lines of the ex-troller could be maintained. As the Jespersons are a shipwright family, the conversion was a relatively easy undertaking, but Eric pointed out that the task can be daunting for someone without woodworking skills. "It's not something that just anybody should take on. Unless the converter can do the work himself, the cost can become prohibitive. Even the annual maintenance overwhelms most people."

With the conversion complete, the boat is serving its purpose well. "We are very pleased with the *San Mateo*," Eric said. "She has exceeded our hopes."

A pristine San Mateo *docked at Nanaimo Harbour almost fifty years after it was launched.*
RYAN WAHL COLLECTION

Philippson, the manager of the North Pacific Cannery, to the parent company, Anglo-British Columbia Packing, explains the company's dilemma and his solution to it. The Wahl Boatyard is a key part of his strategy.

The Wahl Boatyard. About three decades after its inception, the boat shop received a major facelift in the form of a large lean-to structure that was annexed to the front north corner of it (seen here on the right of the building). It contained a grid that could handle larger boats, such as halibut boats, for repair. The addition was a large contributor to the shop's growth from its initial dimensions of 28 feet by 40 feet to its peak size of 165 feet by 185 feet.
MELAINE FILLION COLLECTION

ED. WAHL
Boatyards

SEINE BOATS   PACKERS

HALIBUT BOATS   WORK BOATS

TROLLERS and TUNA BOATS

MARINE WAYS — REPAIRS — ALL KINDS

Dodge Cove, Digby Island

P.O. Box 248, Prince Rupert, B.C.

After the war Ed started advertising his business in Western Fisheries.
COURTESY OF *WESTERN FISHERIES* MAGAZINE

THE ANGLO-BRITISH COLUMBIA PACKING
COMPANY, LIMITED
H. Bell-Irving & Co. Limited, Agents
Vancouver, BC

North Pacific Cannery
Aug. 13, 1957
H. Bell-Irving & Co. Ltd.

Dear Sir:

Received your letter of July 31st in answer to my letter of
May 23rd in which I explained the need for boats. During the
last few years we have definitely gone back[ward] in production by not having kept up our fleet to the standard set by
those companies that have been setting the pace and building
many expensive boats both for rent and sale. This is catching
up with us now and other repercussions are showing, one
of which is that Nelson Bros. who have a very modern and
expensive fleet have offered at least two of our fishermen new
boats and have offered them prices for their old boats which
I think is far too high ...

In my opinion we should get at least ten boats for next
year. Four boats (for rent), 32 ft with Chrysler Ace engines.
Price about $6,000. Four boats from Stoltz or similar, price
approximately $10,000. Two boats 35 ft from Wahl, price
approximately $7,000.

Ed Wahl will complete the small boat for $6,800 and the
35-ft boat for $8,400. I would much rather buy the boats
complete than fuss around completing them but figure that
we save from $500 to $750 by doing it. We are, by the way,
the only ones that do that on any scale except for Sunnyside
and Cassiar, both of [which] get a few Ed Wahl boats. If you
would rather have them completed and bought that way, I do
not anticipate that it will be difficult to arrange.

In direct answer to your questions:

(1) When I say that we need ten new boats every year, I mean that there is a normal depreciation on these boats of about eight percent. Also boats go out of date and, unless you build modern boats, your whole fleet is out of date in a very few years. This is for the whole fleet rental and purchase.

(2) My opinion is that if it were possible it would be best if everyone owned their own boat. Just how that could be done here I do not know. Until a solution can be found we will have to rent, hoping to get sale for some of them and payments down and regularly.

(3) The small 30-foot boats should be taken out of service as soon as possible. We are the only ones using them to any extent and most of them are ten years or older. Most of them were built in 1945 and 1946. We have about twenty-three of them rented from here and there are another twenty wholly or partly owned by the fishermen.

(4) It would be very worthwhile to get out a plan and specification for a suitable boat, and some boats could be built under such a plan. They could not be all built so as the boats would be either too cheap or too expensive for different men as, if they want to buy a boat, they have their own ideas. It would sure save us some headaches if we could buy the boats complete to our specifications.

(5) To continue on here with any degree of success, we have to have new boats every year. Just how many would be required for us to survive I cannot tell but would say that a minimum of ten would be necessary but upwards to fifteen would be better ...

Yours truly,

O. Philippson[1]

---

[1] Letter courtesy of Rare Books and Special Collections Division, University of British Columbia Library.

Rodney Philippson, the nephew of Ole Philippson, recalled that the Wahl Boatyard "put out an all-round good workboat. My uncle was one of the major buyers of them—I think he started buying them as early as 1945. From what I remember, we needed about ten a year to keep the fleet up, between boats retiring and smashing up on the rocks."

Aside from trollers, gillnetters and halibut boats, the Wahl Boatyard produced other types during the 1950s, albeit on a much smaller scale. The earliest recorded seiner—and one of the smallest, if not the smallest—to come out of the Wahl Boatyard was the 36-foot by 14-foot drum seiner *Lawn Hill*, built in 1952 for a Dodge Cove fisherman.

CHAPTER FIVE

A NEW YARD OPENS,
A CHAPTER CLOSES

As the fishing industry grew stronger toward the end of the 1950s, North Coast boat shops were under steady pressure to produce a continuous supply of new boats. Fortunately for the fishermen, Wahl Boatyard was not the only boat works in town during those years.

Norman Murdoch McLean, the first non-Japanese boat builder to come to the area, had established his shop in the Cameron Cove slough (better known as Cow Bay) at the north end of Prince Rupert in 1910. In the beginning he confined himself to building small boats, but after moving his business to the waterfront, he produced larger boats, including packers, seiners and halibut boats. One of these, the *Lysekil*, which he built in 1925, was the largest halibut boat ever built in Cow Bay. A year later McLean moved his shop to its present location at Seal Cove, just around the corner from Cow Bay, and from that point on the shop was kept so busy with repairs that there was no time to build boats. McLean Shipyard is now Prince Rupert's oldest continuously operating boatyard and, like that of the Wahl family, it has always been a family-run business.

Although all the Japanese Canadian boat builders in

the Prince Rupert area had been interned during World War II, several of them returned after the war and most of their reopened businesses were clustered in the Cameron Cove slough. The most famous of these builders was Sam Matsumoto, who went on to become a BC industry leader in the construction of aluminum commercial fishing vessels. Judo (Jack) Tasaka, a fisherman and prominent gillnet boat builder, had supplied boats for a couple of Skeena River canneries before the war. When he returned in 1950, he set up shop at Port Edward, just south of Prince Rupert. In the span of five decades Jack and his two sons built close to two hundred boats, all or most of which were gillnetters. Their unique lines were greatly admired.

The empty shops of the Japanese Canadian builders who didn't return to Prince Rupert after the war were soon occupied by non-Japanese. One of these was Ole Wick, who previously had been boat building at Oona River. In his new Cow Bay shop he built about a boat a year. His sons Ralph and John eventually took over the business, maintaining the same rate of production into the 1970s. (When Henry Wahl married their sister Violet, Ralph and John became Henry's brothers-in-law. Ralph worked with Henry at the Wahl Boatyards during the winter months of the early 1960s.) Other non-Japanese boat-building companies that came into Cow Bay after World War II were Crawley & Didricksen and Kaien Industries.

John Group was a millwright who operated a productive lumber mill at Oona River that was a large source of lumber for Wahl Boatyard, but he was also a famous local boat builder who owned the Porcher Island Boatyard. It was the most productive boat shop ever to operate in Oona River, building about ninety vessels in thirty years.

R odney Philippson assessed the quality of work of all the local boat builders before he asked the Wahls to build his 36-foot gillnetter *BC Harvester* in 1960. "I was looking for an economical boat and not a yacht to fish off. I guess I had a choice between Tasaka, Bob Johnson—he built the *Silver Token* in 1958—and the Wahls. I chose Wahl because of the practicality, price and quality of what you're getting for your dollar. Money was a little different then and we felt that the Wahls were more what we wanted. Tasaka was a little more streamlined and fancier from what I can recall and maybe a third more [in price] or something like that. Another builder that had an impact on boat building in the area is Edgar Snidal from Cassiar Cannery [Cassiar Packing Co.]. He built boats back in the late forties and early fifties. He was one of the first builders to use a transom stern."

Most of Group's boats, like those of the Wahls and Tasaka, went to the Skeena River canneries.

Together these boatyards could meet most of the local demand for new fishboats, but after the Prince Rupert Drydock and Shipyard closed in 1954, the area had too few repair facilities. The Prince Rupert Drydock had stood since 1916 at the north end of the waterfront and, when it opened for business, was the largest one of its kind in North America. Its initial purpose had been the construction of freighters and large war vessels such as minesweepers, but between the wars it supported the fishing fleet by building new boats and servicing existing ones. When work slacked off in the years following World War II, the drydock was closed and then towed south to a new owner.

This left only McLean Shipyard in Seal Cove and Wahl Boatyard in Dodge Cove doing repairs for Prince Rupert area fishermen. The desperate need for more repair and maintenance facilities finally drove the Wahl family to

Sketch of the Prince Rupert Harbour and north end of Dodge Cove, showing the two Wahl boat-yards and sawmill. ILLUSTRATION BY TIA MCLENNAN

Government Wharf

expand its business to give it more scope to both build and repair boats. For the level of expansion the Wahls had in mind, however, they knew they would need to build a completely new boatyard. The next question was where to build it. Strategically, a location at Prince Rupert made the most sense because they could take advantage of the railway for the delivery of goods. And ideally the new location would be right across the harbour from Dodge Cove to minimize travel time between the two boatyards. Fairview Bay, at the south end of Prince Rupert, was the preferred location.

The exact spot on which to set the foundation was a small stretch of beach between the Prince Rupert Fishermen's Co-operative fish processing plant, generally known as the Co-op, and its breakwater. A large fleet of fishing boats docked at that end of the waterfront and they were all potential customers for a new boatyard. Adjacent to Fairview Bay was the Canadian National Railway (CNR) line; its proximity would allow efficient delivery to the new boatyard of lumber and supplies shipped from the south. In early 1959 the $100,000 project kicked off. The

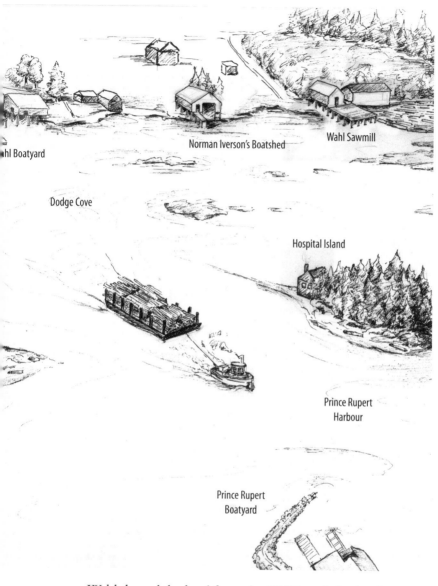

hl Boatyard

Norman Iverson's Boatshed

Wahl Sawmill

Dodge Cove

Hospital Island

Prince Rupert
Harbour

Prince Rupert
Boatyard

Wahls leased the land from the CNR and obtained permits from the city for the construction of a hundred-foot by hundred-foot foundation and shed. Lumber for the new boatyard was cut at the Wahl sawmill and a contractor was lined up to build both the foundation and shed.

The Prince Rupert Boatyard as it looked originally. On the cradle is Silver Bounty, *built by Sam Matsumoto.*
COURTESY OF THE WRATHALL COLLECTION, PRINCE RUPERT CITY & REGIONAL ARCHIVES AND MUSEUM OF NORTHERN BC

Like the Wahl Boatyard at Dodge Cove, the new one—named Prince Rupert Boatyard—at Fairview Bay was designed with one building/launching floor on its north side plus a stall on the south side. The boat-building process would be the same as at the other boatyard— the hull would be constructed on the building floor, launched and then brought into a stall for the remaining construction. But both the building floor and the 100-foot by 38-foot cradle were made larger than those at the Wahl Boatyard, enabling the Wahls to build and repair much larger hulls than they had been able to handle previously.

The centrepiece of the new boatyard was a device of unique design that would truly exploit the under-supply of servicing facilities in the area. Instead of building a traditional one-boat-at-time cradle, a multi-boat cradle was built … This introduced a puzzle, however—how do you get boats off and on the cradle without having to move the other boats already on the cradle? The solution: a split-cradle design.

The split-cradle had three sections that could be split apart and moved separately. Typically the lowest section (closest to the water) was for short-term jobs like copper painting and minor repair work, so it moved steadily up and down. The middle section was for moderate repair jobs—for example, replacing planks or recaulking—that took a little more time. The top section was for very time-consuming work like constructing a cabin or performing a major rebuild. Each section of the cradle was wide enough for two small boats so conceivably the whole cradle could hold six small boats at once.

The November 1959 issue of *Western Fisheries* explained that the cradle design was a West Coast boat-yard innovation:

An innovation in cradles, in this part of the country, at least, is a "split-cradle" whereby only the outer portion need be used for hauling in smaller boats. In this way, boats needing extensive caulking may be left undisturbed, while others may be caulked and painted as fast as time permits. The cradle is hauled by a 30-hp General Electric motor, operating a winch through a Morse Marine coupling and reduction gears. Three-quarter-inch wire rope is used with triple blocks and a half-inch wire rope for hauling the cradle outwards. This is necessary because of the easy gradient.

The 50-foot Searcher, *built in 1963, on her launch day.* ERNEST AND KAY WAHL COLLECTION

According to Malcolm Elder, the cradle could easily handle an 80-foot or 100-foot boat if it wasn't too heavy. But Henry Wahl was confident the cradle could carry a 250-ton ship.

"When is Ed Wahl's new shop opening?" fishermen asked as they waited for the boatyard to be completed. In the end, even though construction was not finished, the work that was piling up motivated the family to open the business early, in October 1959. This marked a new era in the Wahl family's business and, with the fishing fleet in great need of this type of repair facility, no one doubted that it would be as successful as the Dodge Cove Boatyard.

The plan was to build five trollers at the new boat-yard that first winter and the first one completed was the 40-foot *Lori Anne*. Initially fifteen men were employed, with some crew members coming over from Wahl Boatyard, and the shop ran full shifts because an imme-diate and steady flow of boats was coming in for painting and repairs. They included Arne Husoy's *Fredelia III*, Albert Kiistner's *Pillar Bay*, Henry Bell-Irving's *Mylor I* and the Co-op packer *Challenger*, although hauling up this very large packer was no doubt an anxious but exciting moment for the Wahls and their crew. They did a major

Melvin Closter, who had started working for Ed Wahl in 1944, was the last employee to move over to the Prince Rupert Boatyard when it opened, and transporting the crews back and forth between the two boatyards on the company workboat became his job. After twenty years working for the Wahls, Melvin had to leave the boatyards for health reasons, but if you ask anyone who worked alongside him, they will say he was one of the most loyal, hard-working and diligent workers the Wahl boatyards ever employed.

alcolm Elder: "When I started at the Prince Rupert Boatyard, about five guys were hired, I guess. They were finishing carpenters, a couple of rough carpenters, a welder and two of the Wahls—Henry and Ernest. Bobby was in charge of the other [boatyard]." Malcolm had started at the Wahl Boatyard a few years earlier and jumped over to the Prince Rupert Boatyard when it opened. After that, he divided his time between the two yards. His other job at the Prince Rupert Boatyard was night watchman, which involved firing up the boiler for the steambox in the morning. "Being young and alert, for the privilege of living there, I'd keep an eye on things and keep the boiler going. The main thing was to get up in the morning and light it if they were going to be steaming because I wouldn't know what they were going to do that day. Then during the day if I was doing something else, someone else would go and throw some wood in."

rebuild on the dragger *Zenardi* and the *Five Princes*. Erling Wick's *Dovre B* came in for a new wheelhouse, but the highlight of the early servicing jobs was the addition of ten feet to the length of Carl Rosang's well-known seiner *Oldfield*, originally built in 1935. It also received a new stern and pilothouse.

Ed Wahl Retires

Initially Ed Wahl had planned to retire before the new boatyard was built but waited instead until it was operational before officially passing the torch to his sons. Henry became the manager of this boatyard and, to prepare for his new role, he moved his family from Dodge Cove to Prince Rupert. Ernest had already moved to Prince Rupert and would now help to manage operations there, as well as share designing and building duties. Reidar eventually moved to Prince Rupert, too. Operation of the

Wahl Boatyard at Dodge Cove was turned over to Bobby, who remained there, as did Iver and Roald.

Even after his sons had taken up their new roles, Ed retired only partially, much to the chagrin of his family. He had been building boats for thirty-five years and he found letting go difficult, despite constant shoulder and knee pain—he had hurt his knee in the early twenties while logging on Vancouver Island and since then it had been a continual source of discomfort. He'd already been forced

The 42-foot by 12-foot troller Miss Pacific No. 1, *built in 1962. Noticeable in this photo is the pronounced bow flare on the right. Bow flares became a standard coastwide design practice in the early 1950s. A bow flare enables water shedding in a head sea, for a "dry boat"; the more pronounced the flare the better the water shedding. In the early 1960s the Wahl troller received even more flare in the bow and a more rounded forward deck, almost to the shape of a semicircle.* RYAN WAHL COLLECTION

to give up planking and the other more demanding jobs, leaving him with only a few tasks he could still do, such as fitting the bow stems. To make work easier for him, his sons set up a bench he could use for support, but it wasn't long before he gave in to his family's demands to quit.

He sold the home that he and Mary had built on Dodge Cove to Bobby and for a time he lived in the original family home above the Wahl Boatyard with May Hutchinson, who had come as housekeeper after Mary died and stayed to become Ed's partner. He then embarked on a house-building project in Langley, close to the Fraser River.

For Ed's whole life, aside from work and family he had taken great pleasure in spending time on his own and had made a point of periodically going on solo excursions all over the United States in his Oldsmobile Rocket 88. Now he bought himself a new Chrysler Royal automobile in which he planned to take May on long holidays, though he jokingly told his boys that he bought it only so that he could come back and check on them once in a while. "Yeah, I can just see it," Iver said. "He'd be coming up with a tool box in the back seat and going back to work!"

For many years he had built skiffs as a hobby and, according to Iver, he always took in young fellows to apprentice with him. "Oh, he built lots of [skiffs] and he always had a young fellow to help him, you know ... showed him how to do it. He really liked that. That's how he wanted to retire," Iver said.

Later on down his retirement road Ed planned to go sport fishing as well. Ed had owned his share of speedboats and cabin cruisers over the years, one of his favourites being the cruiser that his sons built for him. "He had a fast boat but it wasn't very big," Iver explained, "and there wasn't much heat in it so it was a poor boat in the winter. So we made up our minds that we were going to build Dad a boat and then we wouldn't have to worry about him. We built a 35-foot boat like a fishing boat, just the way he wanted it. We put a brand new Crown Chrysler [engine] in it. Was he ever happy! He really liked that boat." Despite what the boat meant to him, Ed's giving nature got the best of him. "The manager from Sunnyside Cannery came to Dad and said, 'You got to sell me that boat. It's the boat I've been dreaming of for years and years.' Dad didn't want to part with it but he was so good-hearted, you know, so he finally broke down and sold him the boat." Now, perhaps, it was time for a new cruiser yacht for sportfishing.

All Ed Wahl's future plans were shattered, however, when he suffered severe pain at the beginning of March 1961. With Henry and May at his side, he was rushed to Vancouver. The diagnosis was cancer and due to its wide-spread nature the doctors could do nothing but send him home. "He had never been sick in his life," Iver said. "He was healthy as can be. He had a heart on him like a bull." Surrounded by family and friends, Ed Wahl, a man who had been the personification of kindness and fortitude, died on March 19, 1961. He was sixty-five.

"Ed Wahl was a quiet man and easy to get along with," recalled Melvin Closter, the longest-serving employee at the Wahl Boatyards. "New workers were always given a chance. When he died, I felt lost, as I was used to seeing him every morning. The place seemed empty without him."

CHAPTER SIX

SIX SONS TO CARRY ON

Malcolm Elder, whose talent of observation in the boatyard was invaluable in researching this book, described the Wahl brothers as having "a lot of similarities between them. They weren't pushy guys and one thing they didn't like was physical violence. They weren't violent men at all. But mainly, they had a lot of talent and a good eye." But while it is true that the brothers shared some common traits, at the end of my research when someone said to me with a smile, "All of Ed's sons

Four of the Wahl boys in a relaxed moment at Roald and Violet's home. Left to right: *Bobby, Roald, Henry and Iver.* ROALD AND VIOLET WAHL COLLECTION

were great and they were all a little different," I had to smile, too. It was a great summary of the individual skills and character that each of them brought to the boatyard.

Being the eldest, Henry was expected to follow in his father's footsteps, not only to become a master shipwright but also to oversee the operation of all the family businesses. He had accomplished all of this while still in his early twenties. But in addition to being a great boat builder, Henry was universally known as a highly intelligent, friendly and focussed individual. "He was definitely a bright fellow," Malcolm said. "He had talent and he had the ability to concentrate. For most of us it's patchy, but Henry could concentrate and be oblivious to what was going on around him when he was into a job. I think you could have walked up and kicked him and he wouldn't have noticed because he would be concentrating so intensely." But Henry was also known as a "crackerjack" and a "daredevil" and could never have been categorized as a conservative shipwright. "Henry needed the challenge, something different," commented Malcolm. Henry's biggest challenge came in the lengthening of the *Sunnfjord*, which went down in the history books as one the most notable engineering feats in marine history.

Custom-built boats are designed according to the owner's specifications, based on what he feels he needs at the time. Boats built "on spec," on the other hand, are designed by the builder and any subsequent changes are made at the expense of the buyer. Regardless of who sets the boat specifications, however, invariably the boat owner will eventually want to make changes, generally prompted by the innate human tendency to want to "keep up with the Joneses." For fishboats this means updates that range from the relatively simple such as a new paint scheme, which the owner usually does himself, to major additions, for example, adding a dodger to extensive renovations such as building a new stern or cabin. But the one change that has always been in its own category because of its radical nature is extending the length of the boat. The driver for this alteration is easy to grasp: it is the best way to stay competitive in the fishing industry without purchasing a new boat.

The boat-lengthening process is simple in concept but very precise and complex in execution. For the Wahls, although the process varied, it always followed these basic steps: the boat was braced high enough to get the old keel out, the old keel was removed and the new keel was installed, the boat was chain-sawed at the mid-point down to the keel, and the stern section was pulled back along the new keel so that the new midship section could be framed and planked. The result was a boat with more deck space and a larger fish hold capacity, the latter being the change the boat owner wanted most because it would instantly improve his bottom line. A side benefit to the alteration was that working other fisheries now became possible; the owner who was once excluded from a particular fishery because his boat was too small could now join in. A good example of this—something the Wahls did numerous times—was extending an ordinary troller to a length suitable for the halibut fishery.

The Wahl family became very adept at this lengthening operation though it was not without its challenges. The greatest challenge—because of the boat's size—was the 11-foot lengthening of the well-known 72-foot by 20-foot-½-inch herring seiner *Sunnfjord*, which was capable of carrying about one hundred tons of fish. Sam Matsumoto built it in 1957 and, when it was brought to the Wahls for lengthening, John Haugan was its skipper.

The improved Sunnfjord *at Victoria, delivering a load of herring packed in from the San Juan Islands.* JACK PRINCE COLLECTION

The Sunnfjord *inside the boatyard.*
JACK PRINCE COLLECTION

It was Henry Wahl's job to engineer this task and his plan was to cut the boat in half as usual then slide the aft section along the new keel by pulling the cradle sections apart. But as if the complications of the job weren't stressful enough, the owners were urging that the job be done quickly so that the boat could be returned to fishing as soon as possible. As well, Henry had to fight off skepticism from other marine professionals who believed the extended boat would sink when fully loaded.

The *Sunnfjord* was hauled up onto the cradle in September 1963 and the momentous job began. At the end of the process, the already very large boat had grown to 83 feet and, according to Ernest, could carry 150 tons with 10 inches of freeboard. With the success of the job came many accolades, including a glowing report from *Western Fisheries*: "The yard is to be commended on a big job well done in a short time … this will be worth watching."

"We cut her in half and put eleven feet in," Ernest said. "Eleven feet! Henry argued with the steamboat inspector who was going to stop us doing it. In the end he let us do it but Henry had to put the load line mark on it. It happened that the steamboat inspector was in town when the boat came in with its first load of herring. Henry told him to come down to the dock right away. When he got there, Henry said to him, 'There you are! There's the boat you said wouldn't pack 150 ton of herring.'"

In 1963, the Sunnfjord *was lengthened by an impressive 11 feet. Here, the new midship is going in.* JACK PRINCE COLLECTION

he Wahls lengthened many boats, among them these:
- 1946: the halibut boat *Selma H* by 7 feet to 48 feet.
- 1955: the *Neptune II* by 9 feet.
- 1956: the halibut boat *Viking I* by 7 feet.
- 1959: the seiner *Oldfield* by 10 feet.
- 1960: the *Flora H*, owned by the Canadian Fishing Company, by 7 feet. At the same time the deck was raised by 10 inches.
- 1961: the *Miss Margot* by 8 feet.
- 1966: the troller *Succeed* by 3½ feet to 41½ feet.
- 1969: the 40-foot troller *Marble Isle* by 8 feet.

"It didn't take very long," Iver said. "It was a hurry-up job on account of the herring [fishery]. I'll never forget that, boy! It's never been done on this coast before. It's been done in Norway."

"It was a hell of a tough job," Malcolm Elder recounted, "and it could have ended in disaster. Some boatyard down south tried to lengthen and widen a boat at the same time. This was considered a virtual engineering impossibility. It wasn't successful."

"I don't think a lot of people realized what a big job it actually was," Art Stace-Smith said. "Some people say it wasn't impossible, but I tell you it was a *big* undertaking. You know one slight screw-up ... which did happen once at a shipyard down in Vancouver ... They were lengthening a boat that size and they made a bit of a mistake. They never got over it and it damn near broke 'em. It was costly to get the boat back in shape because they had wasted hundreds of hours. When [the Wahls] cut the *Sunnfjord*, it went off without a flaw."

To even consider undertaking an operation like lengthening, you first need a leader with the guts to do

Iver on playing the accordion: "I picked it up on my own. We had lots of free time because there was no TV in the house. Henry played it first and I started with the mouth organ. I liked it so much after he started to play it that I decided to buy myself an old Chromatic accordion."
MARY WAHL COLLECTION

it. If it hadn't been for Henry, the Wahl family probably would never have tried it. But long before the *Sunnfjord* job, he had been honing his lengthening skills on smaller boats. One was a 40-foot boat that he lengthened by 8 feet. "And he was good at putting the keel in, too," Ernest said. "He put a new keel into a 72-footer in seven days. I don't think anybody else could ever do that. It would have taken the outfits down south two months to do it."

Outside of the boat shop all the brothers fished, some more than others. For a boat-building family, it was a natural second job to fall into and, according to Iver, it was more than just another source of income for the family; it was an opportunity to get out of a hectic and stressful environment that often bordered on madness. "We took three months off in the summertime," Iver said. "That was

The *Lance:* Something New in a Halibut Boat

Foster Husoy's halibut boat, the *Lance*, constructed at the Prince Rupert Boatyard, made headlines in the summer of 1963 before it even hit the water. In the July issue of *Western Fisheries* it was noted that its "proposed layout for seven bunks on deck" would be "an innovation for a boat in the 55-foot class." As Foster explained to me, the design had taken Henry and him some serious brainstorming.

"We sat down and worked it out together," Foster said. "I wanted crew accommodations for six men above deck—usually the bunks are down below and I didn't want that. I tried to cut costs as much as I could to get the other things that I wanted. Like in the galley, Henry was going to go flat-out fancy and I told him you don't need all that stuff because this is only where the guys are going to sit and eat. We don't have to eat in such a high-class restaurant! But you could give Henry a problem about that kind of stuff and he would eventually figure it out. Sometimes he would get really queer and other times he was a bloody genius. But then that goes for all of us, I guess! So

anyway, he sat down and figured it out and we got what we wanted."

Foster had full confidence in the performance of his new boat and he backed up his conviction by heading straight for Alaska's worst areas. "You know, that was the best sea boat I've ever been on. We lived through some terrible weather up in the Gulf of Alaska. We were actually in a 125-mile-an-hour gale up there and she rode it out fine. A lot of those big American schooners had problems in that storm. Some of them shifted their wheelhouses and one actually had its house taken off."

The *Lance* gave Foster Husoy some highly successful years in the halibut and herring fisheries before facing its last storm in the late 1960s. They were herring fishing at the mouth of the Portland Canal, thirty-five miles north of Prince Rupert. "It was December one year and blowing a forty-five-mile-an-hour northeasterly. We got almost a full load of herring and it shifted on us. The crew had left the centreboards out and that allowed the load to shift. She rolled over onto her side and luckily we all got off and into the life raft. About ten minutes later the life raft turned over, so we all had to get out from underneath it and get on top. I wanted to flip it back over again, but the guys refused so we climbed back on top of it. By this time we were all soaking wet but we stayed warm by huddling together.

"Then we saw the *Standard Service*. She was coming down from Skagway and was just off the northern tip of Dundas. We managed to flag her down with my bright orange life jacket. Were we ever glad to see it!

"We spent five and a half hours riding on an overturned life raft and we just about froze to death but everyone came out of it fine. A guy in the Coast Guard up in Alaska told me that he couldn't believe that we could survive that long. Only one [crew member] got any ill effects at all. I didn't realize it at the time, but he'd sort of drifted off to one side by himself and had fallen asleep. I hauled him back in with the rest of us. He ended up in the hospital, verging on pneumonia."

The Lance *docked in Prince Rupert.*
JACK PRINCE COLLECTION

our holiday. Dad always left for halibut fishing on May 12." Henry was regarded as a good fisherman, too. After skippering the *Island Queen* with much success, he owned several boats including the *Edward Wahl*, the *Breezeway* and the *Tracey Lee* (named after his granddaughter). But he typically fished a boat for only a few seasons before selling it. "I fished with Henry every year he went halibut fishing," Iver said. "I had fished with different guys and was actually an old, old halibut fisherman when I went with Henry. He couldn't set a hook when I first went with him. So I taught him. Henry was a good fisherman. Very, very good. Yeah, he always made money. Of course, he had been fishing with Dad and he was top-notch, too.

"The *Edward Wahl* was his first halibut boat. I was courting Mary when he had that. It was quite big, you know—46 feet. It was a dandy sea boat. We had six men on it—the same number of guys that we had on the *Island Queen*. One time we were fishing up at Shag Rock and a hell of a southeaster come up. Of course, we couldn't go out—well, I guess we could have but we didn't. Henry said, 'That's enough of this so let's go anchor up.' So we went and anchored up in this harbour where there was this big whaling station. As soon as we anchored, we went down below and then the boat started leaning over. We hollered out, 'Well, boys, it looks like we're here for a while!' We were just about high and dry but we were all right. We took a shovel and a couple of buckets and filled them plum full of clams—beautiful, nice, big white clams.

"I don't think he had that boat for two seasons. He sold it right in the middle of fishing season for $12,000 and then he built himself a gillnet boat—*Fiesta* was the name of it. Him and I fished halibut on that, too. He had it for two or three seasons."

Iver was especially close to Henry. Growing up, the two had been virtually inseparable and in our many discussions, Iver always had something to say about his older brother. "He was a hell of a swell guy but he didn't take no crap. You treat him right and he'd do anything for you. He only went to grade seven but he sure was a smart man, boy. Navigation, you know, he was really, really into that. He took it up all himself. Salter, he was the head manager for the Canadian Fishing Company and the whole northern area, and he got to know Henry and really took a great liking to him. He was after Henry all the time to run these big fish packers for him. And Henry, he damn near took one but then he changed his mind for some reason. I wish he would have, you know, just to prove to some of these fishermen that he could do it. And Dad, he was kind of disgusted, too, because he wanted to see him do it."

Iver Wahl also became a master shipwright, able to build a boat from a half-model to the final product, but unlike his father and older brother, the only place he felt comfortable was at the core of the business—the building floor. His specialty was plank cutting and that is how most people from the boatyard remember him. "Dad and Henry were hard to beat [at plank cutting]," Iver told me. "But I cut planks for twenty-two years and I never used any templates. I just stood and looked at the boat and then I cut about seven rounds of planking on each side. No measurements. But when I got towards the top, I had to measure the distance so that I only cut so many. I cut up to thirty rounds to finish it. It's easy to make a mistake on the calculation and I made a lot of mistakes and had to start figuring it out all over again. But I never wasted lumber. Sometimes it was really hair-raising, you know. I had to keep the planks coming. You got four guys

Roald, Art Stace-Smith and Iver at Iver and Mary's house in Prince Rupert.
MARY WAHL COLLECTION

[planking], two guys on each side. You had to keep them going."

Malcolm Elder considered Iver "the number one planker. He was an expert at it. He'd be busy cuttin' the planks and maybe a couple of young guys would be putting them on. Every once in a while he'd come down and show them where they had too big of holes between the planks." Art Stace-Smith's best memories were of working with the planking crew with Iver cutting planks. "It was a race to see if you could do as well or better than the previous crew. Battens, ribs and planking would come out of the steambox hot and you would run like hell to place

Ernest, a fine woodworker, was known as the finishing man.
MARY WAHL COLLECTION

it in the boat structure. Everybody hustled and there was pride in a job well done, but the Wahl boys set the pace and worked very hard themselves. The boats were pleasing to the eye. Although there were measurements and patterns, there was a lot of judging by eye and I remember Iver standing by the band saw in a certain spot to judge the shape of the boat and making adjustments accordingly. The caulking mallet was a constant rhythm and set the pace for the whole boat shop. When it stopped it seemed like something was missing."

Because Iver had such a good eye for curves, after the new boatyard was built on Fairview Bay, he would travel over there whenever it came time to craft a new boat's sheer line. "That was my job. I used to go between the Prince Rupert Boatyard and the Wahl Boatyard. Henry sent a guy over to pick me up."

Apart from fishing halibut on various boats, Iver did some trolling on his own to earn extra cash. He was just sixteen when he got his first fishing boat, a troller named *R and I*. He $600 for it with money earned from fishing halibut that summer. "Dad, he was my banker—he looked

Ernest aboard his boat Tracer, *built in 1944, with Hospital Island in the background.* ERNEST AND KAY WAHL COLLECTION

after my money," Iver explained. "And I saw this boat and I wanted it but he said I couldn't buy it. He wouldn't give me my money. He said I was way too young to have a boat. I didn't care because I wanted it. I raised such a stink he had to give in. I got it home and he said, 'You certainly can't go out by yourself.' I said, 'No, Bobby's coming with me.'" Bobby was only twelve at the time.

Iver fished only because the money was good. He never became a high-liner but just broke even. He got more enjoyment out of fixing boats up or fiddling around with their engines. One such boat was the company workboat *WB.* "I bought it from the company and then I completely rebuilt the whole boat. I wanted to put her back to the way she was when we first built her. I changed everything that was damaged or patched up. I threw the engine out and put in a Penta diesel that Ernest got me in Vancouver. We installed a new shaft, new rudder and everything. Just got it the way we really wanted. Damn, that engine ... I really fell in love with it ... ran like a charm."

ERNEST AND KAY WAHL COLLECTION

*Bobby was well known in the
gillnetting circle.*

ROALD AND VIOLET WAHL
COLLECTION.

Ernest was regarded as a great shipwright as well and,
like his father, went about his work in a steady and diligent
fashion. At the two boatyards Ernest and Henry were the
main boat designers and at the Prince Rupert Boatyard
it was usually Henry who built the hull and Ernest who
built the wheelhouse.

"Ernest was an excellent boat builder," Malcolm Elder
said. "He did some very fine work and he was a good
finishing man. If they had a boat sitting up there and
they were putting a house on it, he'd frame the house up
because he could do it so quickly. We had a Norwegian
working there who would go inside and do the cabins—

he was more of a cabinetmaker type—but Ernest could do it, too."

Ernest didn't fish as much as his brothers did. The most vivid memory Iver had of Ernest and boats concerned the 16-foot runabout that Ernest crashed into a rock pile. "It was a wreck when he got it so he had to rebuild it completely," Iver said. "Then he bought himself a brand new 100-hp V8 Ford. It was a nice little engine. It had a clutch on it, a manifold and everything. And boy, did it go! I guess it did a good forty-five miles an hour. He had it for two years before running it over a rock pile. Bobby was with him. They jumped right over the rock pile. Smashed it completely. Well, they're lucky they pulled out of it. A gillnetter came by and picked them up. The crash was so bad the engine was lying there on the rocks. Ernest didn't buy another speedboat after that."

Bobby also rose to rank of master shipwright, specializing in wheelhouses, but his passion was the day-to-day running of the office, so he jumped between wearing coveralls and wearing a business suit. "Every morning he laid out the work and put the men where he wanted them," said Bobby's second wife, Marge. "He just loved all of that boat business—anything to do with it. He also loved the boys to sit down on the boat and talk about all their fishing and everything."

Those who knew Bobby well described him as a very kind and compassionate individual. His interactions with customers exemplified this; for example, if a payment wasn't forthcoming he let the customer keep the boat and pay later instead of cancelling the contract. Marge said, "I've seen times he'd go along the street

Opposite: *Bobby's gillnetter* Golden Crest, *built in 1968.*
ART SWITZER COLLECTION

Viro-K *and* Golden Crest *coming into Dodge Cove.*
ROALD AND VIOLET WAHL COLLECTION

to some kid shining shoes and give him a good tip to help him. Also, he told anybody that needed to redo their steps or had other little jobs around their place to do they could have the material from the sawmill. Most places, you know, need a little upkeep now and then."

Norman Iverson described Bobby as the kind of guy who could talk the pants off a nun. A long-time resident of the Prince Rupert area, Norman became good friends with Bobby through business dealings with the family. "I was half-owner of the sawmill in Oona River and the Wahls were our customers. I sold boat lumber to these guys and, in fact, they got pretty well every bit of boat lumber we produced. I remember one time he came to Oona River because he wanted some boat lumber. He said, 'If you guys can saw 20,000 feet, I'll take it tomorrow.'

"So Bobby was kind of a compadre of mine for the longest time. I don't know how we happened to team up, but he used to be out in Oona River a great deal—like on the weekends he'd come out there and visit—and we got to be great friends about the time that his [first] wife, Katie, got sick [circa 1965]. He used to come out quite a bit then and she used to come out, too, until she couldn't do it anymore."

Norman also owned a small boatyard at Dodge Cove. "One day I was down at the float here at Dodge Cove and I was going to paint my boat because I was getting ready to go fishing, and Bobby came along. He said, 'What are you doing now?' and I said, 'Well, I'm painting the boat.' He said, 'There are lots of people who can paint boats. We need somebody who can drive nails.' They were building the *BC Safari* at that time at the PRB [Prince

Roald and Violet on Viro-K.
ROALD AND VIOLET WAHL COLLECTION

Reidar provided comic relief around the boatyard.
ROALD AND VIOLET WAHL COLLECTION

Rupert Boatyard] and I ended up over there until it was launched and then I went fishing."

With their older brothers already filling the boatyard's management, foreman and designer roles, Roald and Reidar worked with the crew on the assembly line. "I just went by the measurements and built," Roald said. "Henry, Iver and Ernest made the models and designed most of the boats. Bobby did some, too, but they did the most of it. Reidar was a very smart man, but we never had to get into that because they were doing the modelling and we were helping build them. Reidar and I helped rib and plank many boats besides doing many other jobs. That's the way it was. We each had our own part of the business to do." When he returned to the boatyard after twelve years running the family sawmill, Roald, like Bobby, became very adept at constructing wheelhouses. The best way to describe Roald on the job was "steady Eddy." Whether in the boat shop or sawmill he was always solid, by the book, reliable and firm but not pushy. Many say that out of all the brothers, he was most like his dad in demeanour and physical characteristics.

Of all Ed's sons, Roald was one of the busiest fishermen. The first of his boats was *Seafoam* and it was followed by *Provider*, for which Iver built the hull and Roald built the cabin. The third was the *Viro-K*, which had special importance to his family because the name was a combination of the first one or two letters of each family member's name: "Vi" for Roald's wife, Violet, "R" for Roald, "O" for Olav, their son, and "K" for Kathy, their daughter.

Reidar was drawn to the engineering, mechanical and electrical side of the family business. "Give him an old engine or some broken-down electrical appliance and he'd make it run," Iver said. Among Reidar's gillnetters was the *Coney Isle*, which he bought in early 1954.

But Reidar was also a jokester, a prankster, the comic relief of the boatyard. He made the atmosphere there fun and as a result was often accused of doing too much fooling around. "Reidar, he would pull some awful capers," Malcolm Elder said. "There was no end to his stunts. I remember one time a much respected Norwegian troller came in and he wanted a new stem put in his boat because the old one was rotten. Henry got the job. So she's up

In 1967 Art Stace-Smith commissioned the Wahls to build him a 42-foot troller. It was named Kootenay. ART STACE-SMITH COLLECTION

on the front carriage and there's no rush as we've got all winter to do it. There was a lot of work behind it so some of the hard carpenters were put on it and they told Reidar to put the stem in. He takes the old stem out and he makes up the new one, a yellow cedar stem. He gets it all in there and I don't think they'd finished nailing it up when the old Norwegian came in and grabbed Henry. 'Come up on the deck,' he said. So off they go. They look out the front window and here the boat is going this way and the stem is going that way. Reidar didn't get the rabbets on both sides! You see, you rabbet into the stem and they should be opposite to each other all the way down. But they weren't opposite to each other so the stem was cock-eyed. Henry said it isn't going to hurt the performance at all but it's going to drive me crazy. He blew up and went down to one of the hired carpenters, a German guy, and said, 'Take this over and straighten it up.' So there wasn't too much profit made on that one."

"Reidar was so funny," Marge said. "One time he went over to town ... [and coming back] he ran out of gas and I looked out and I thought, what am I seeing? He was in a little boat like the *WB*—but I don't think it was the *WB*—and he was *paddling* his way back. There were so many times that [the boat] was underwater and he'd get it out, dry out the engine and go again."

Everyone who did business with the Wahl brothers had good things to say about them, but those who worked with them knew them best. "They were all fine guys," remembered Norman Iverson. "There wasn't one of them guys that wasn't." Art Stace-Smith regarded them as "the boat builders of the north. There's just no doubt about that. Nobody ever equalled them." But he also knew them as friends. "We downed some home brew and raised a little hell and also did some hunting and sport fishing. We became good friends."

CHAPTER SEVEN

RUNNING FULL TILT

After the Prince Rupert Boatyard opened at Fairview Bay, Henry's leadership abilities were called upon immediately because the bank loan taken out to construct it had to be paid off before any real profit could be made. "Henry was a real hellraiser," Iver said. "He was driving the heck out of everything to pay for it, going day and night. He built a heck of a pile of boats, but he couldn't handle all of them, so I also built them over at the Wahl Boatyard."

In three seasons Henry had paid off the loan, but the pace never slackened after that. Like his father, he had a vision of running the shop like a well-oiled machine, but the machine he had in mind was one constantly in overdrive. He would take on new work even if the shop was already running at full capacity and he turned away jobs only if he absolutely had to. It was this mentality coupled with an ability to provide fast and quality service that made the family's yards a sure bet when it came to getting a quick turnaround. "We're versatile," Henry was quoted as saying. "We'll tackle anything." And it was true, although their yards dealt mostly with commercial boats. Gillnetters, trollers, seiners, packers, combination boats and tugboats were all taken up onto the cradle for servicing.

By positioning their new boatyard right next to the

Co-op at the south end of Prince Rupert, the Wahls had made it part of an already busy centre of activity. The Co-op plant, which had been started by independent North Coast boat owners around the start of the Depression, was a diverse operation. As well as processing the catch, in the spring as the fishing fleet prepared for the coming season, the plant had several grids that provided fishermen with an option for servicing their own boats. In the prime fishing years an the 1960s, fishermen waited in line to

One of the boats built at the old boatyard after the Prince Rupert Boatyard opened was the *Escapade*. In 1960 Leo Carter owned the *Spray No. 1*, which had been built at the Wahl Boatyard in 1948 for Nels Antonsen, but Leo dreamed of fishing off Cape Fairweather in Alaska, so he commissioned the Wahls to build him a new boat. With the specifications he had in mind, no existing templates lying around the shop could be used. His design called for something out of the ordinary. "It was my idea to put the stern timber down in the water and to put the dodger sloping back. And after that, everybody did it," he said. These personal touches added to the already efficient, eye-pleasing Wahl design but the boat's extra length made the new troller look somewhat unconventional.

When the 48-foot by 13-foot *Escapade* was launched in March 1960 from the Wahl Boatyard, it was the largest boat built on the BC coast solely for trolling, but a number of marine architects said it was too big to be effective as a troller. *Western Fisheries* magazine said it looked like "a small Johnstone Strait seiner," though they did note in its favour that "with a beam of 13 feet she has great stability ... Her stern is deep and wide, making her steady in a following sea. Her hold is large, running 3 feet under the house, and is capable of holding 35,000 pounds of salmon and ice."

Carter had wanted his troller built larger than the standard 42-footer to enable him to stay on the grounds for a much longer period and make each trip more profitable. "That was in the back of my mind all those years until I paid the *Spray* off and got some money ahead so I could build the *Escapade*. Everybody called me the craziest kid on the waterfront because they told me, 'That's a small seiner!' They thought I'd completely lost my marbles." But Leo's success with the *Escapade* proved them wrong.

use these grids or to have their boats hauled up into the Prince Rupert Boatyard, while others were docked at the Co-op floats to receive a fresh coat of paint. Then, like the ebb and flow of the tides, as the fishing season drew closer a steady stream of boats began heading out to the fishing grounds and, by the season's opening day, the waterfront was left empty.

Most boatyards saw little, if any, action during the summer. Not so the Wahl boatyards. They rarely took a break even during the natural summer slack time simply because Henry liked to keep things humming all year round. Despite the huge temptation for the younger men to leave the shop in summer for the lucrative fishing industry, he managed to keep a small crew on not only for servicing but also for new construction. "They had not a bad program of taking in apprentices," Malcolm Elder said. "But you see, the problem with these apprentices was trying to keep them. Some of them put in a couple of years and the company was treating them pretty good, I'd say, compared to the usual idea of apprenticeship. But some of their pals would come rolling in off a fishing boat with $5000 sticking out of their hip pockets from just a short trip. 'What am I doing here?' they'd say."

At the end of each fishing season, the fleet would return and then remain idle throughout the winter and this was when the boatyards were at their busiest. Henry would supplement the crews with unemployed fishermen and the Wahl Boatyards would head into a full winter program of new construction. Between orders for gill-netters and trollers alone, the shop remained constantly busy. The trollers rolled off the assembly line especially fast, which undoubtedly made the 1960s the "golden age" of trollers. Those built by the Wahls came in lengths of 38, 40 and 42 feet, the latter being the most popular. Orders for halibut boats, packers and seiners came in less frequently.

During the late 1960s, improvements in the form of add-ons were being made to the Prince Rupert Boatyard. Work began with the addition of a small dock

Below left: *The 40-foot by 12-foot Wahl troller* Nordon, *built in 1963. Even as a silhouette on a gloomy day, the shape of a Wahl boat is unmistakable.*
CHRIS FORDHAM COLLECTION

Below right: *The* Bonnie B No. 1, *the* Miss Janine *and* Storm Prince *made the cover of* Western Fisheries, *together and individually.* COURTESY OF *WESTERN FISHERIES* MAGAZINE

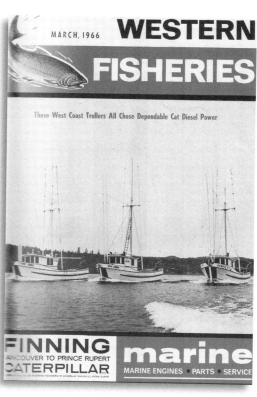

These are the known seiners built in the 1960s at the Wahl boatyards:

- 1960: 46-foot by 15-foot *Scaner*, launched on June 21. Designed and built by Henry and Ernest. Powered by a 165-hp General Motors marine diesel.
- 1963: 49-foot drum seiner, name unknown.
- 1964: 46-foot by 15-foot drum seiner, name unknown.
- 1967: 65-foot *Western Viking*.
- 1968: 54-foot *Qitonsta*.
- 1969: 54-foot *Velmar*.

Nanaimo Trio of Trollers

In 1964 three near-sister ships built for three Nanaimo customers all made the cover of *Western Fisheries* magazine, individually and together. These "pretty boats" had all been built during the previous winter in the Wahl boatyards, but though similar they were not identical.

Butch Neave's *Storm Prince*, built by Henry, was the largest and most highly powered of the three, measuring 42 feet by 12 feet by 5 feet and fitted with a 120-hp Caterpillar diesel. It was one of only a few fishing boats that earned *Western Fisheries'* "Pick of the Crop" honours in 1964. Bernie Bennett's *Bonnie B No. 1* (now *Surf No. 1*), also built by Henry, was a foot shorter and a foot narrower and was powered by an 80-hp Cat. Jack Reinhard's *Miss Janine*, which Iver built, was a foot shorter than the *Bonnie B* but had the same width and depth and carried the same power.

The Miss Janine, *built by Iver.*
COURTESY OF NORTH PACIFIC PAPERS, NORTH PACIFIC CANNERY NHS, PORT EDWARD, BC

The Bonnie B No. 1 (now Surf No. 1), *built by Henry.*
COURTESY OF NORTH PACIFIC PAPERS, NORTH PACIFIC CANNERY NHS, PORT EDWARD, BC

The Storm Prince, *built by Henry, was "Pick of the Crop" in 1964.*
COURTESY OF NORTH PACIFIC PAPERS, NORTH PACIFIC CANNERY NHS, PORT EDWARD, BC

with a ramp, then on each side of the main shed lean-to stalls were built that would house boats as big as trollers. Finally, the cradle was upgraded to handle greater loads, which allowed the airport ferry and large tugboats to be hauled up.

The Prince Rupert Boatyard after extensive upgrades.. RYAN WAHL COLLECTION

Frank Amstutz and His Wahl Boats

In a fishing career that spanned more than thirty years, Frank Amstutz had two well-known Wahl trollers—first the *Fan Isle*, built in 1961, and then the *Ocean Roamer*, built in 1965. Both boats made headlines—but for different reasons.

Frank's fishing career had started in 1936 when, at the age of twenty-two, he raised an old 28-foot logging boat from its watery graveyard, patched it up to make it seaworthy, replaced damaged planks and put on a new cabin. "I said if the thing comes up, I'll patch it up and reuse it. Well, it came up. I went fishing with that thing and I never thought anything of it." *Alkie*—as he called it—wasn't the Cadillac of the fishing fleet, but in Frank's first—and only—season on it he trolled by hand and made $500, which "was a fortune at the time." He had his next boat, the *Yvonne*, for only one season as well.

Frank next set his sights on fishing in Hecate Strait, the body of water between Prince Rupert and the Queen Charlotte Islands, where "the cohos were like grapes." The strait's reputation for strong tides, constantly shifting winds, thick fog and overall rough fishing conditions wasn't enough to scare him off, but he wasn't crazy either—he needed to procure a boat that would hold up in that environment. He knew of the Wahls' reputation for building not only sturdy, seaworthy boats but "nice-lookin' boats" as well. "I wrote to Ed to order a boat and he wrote back and said he's sorry but he couldn't take [my order] because he was blocked solid. It was one of those 34-footers I was trying to get."

Frank's order was subsequently accepted at Stanley Park Shipyard in Vancouver and in 1938 the 36-foot *Redfern I* was launched. "We made one trip with the *Redfern I* in Hecate Strait," Frank's wife, Blanche, said, "and Frank decided he was going to need

Frank and Blanche Amstutz.
FRANK AND BLANCHE AMSTUTZ COLLECTION

a bigger boat. In April 1945 we sold the house [in Vancouver] with all our furniture except my sewing machine and we moved to Rupert. We couldn't rent a house so we bought an old house up on 8th Avenue. No furnace, just an oil stove in the kitchen."

They had a new boat built by local builder Ole Wick at his shop in Cow Bay. It was originally named *Stalin*, but because of the backlash that the name created, Frank changed the name to *Pride*. (Frank can't remember why he was so brazen in picking the original name but believes it was done on a dare.) Now behind the wheel of a larger boat, he could fish virtually anywhere in Hecate Strait, regardless of the weather conditions.

But in 1952 Frank had to quit fishing for health reasons and the Amstutzs moved back to Vancouver and then to Nanaimo in 1957, where Frank kept busy building houses. But after a five-year absence from commercial fishing, he was back on the phone to the Wahls again, hoping this time they would accept his order. By luck, Henry had just finished a boat but had no buyer for it. At 42 feet by 12 feet 2 inches by 6 feet 5 inches, it was much bigger than the *Pride*, which is what Frank and Blanche were looking for. "When [the wind] blew," Blanche said, "you were a little more comfortable in a bigger boat." Frank threw in his favourite marine engine, a Caterpillar. The launching as reported in the April 1961 issue of *Western Fisheries*:

> Thursday, March 23rd, was another big day at the Prince Rupert Boatyard, operated by Wahls at Fairview Bay, when the new 42-foot troller built

The Fan Isle, *built in 1961 for Nanaimo resident Frank Amstutz.* FRANK AND BLANCHE AMSTUTZ COLLECTION

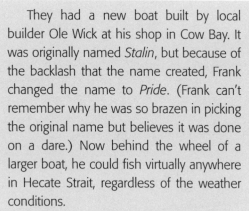

for Frank Amstutz was launched and taken on her trials. Although details of the trials are not known at present, it is understood that the new boat showed a wonderful turn of speed, and was quite acceptable to the proud owner ... With approximately 70 people in attendance, the christening was performed by Mrs. W.J. Currie. [The boat] was named *Fan Isle*.

Early tests were positive, as reported in the June 1961 issue of *Western Fisheries*:

[Frank Amstutz's] new vessel averages 10.5 knots on trials in Vancouver Harbour, and showed good stability on high-speed turns. The skipper was very happy with her manoeuverability at high or low speeds. This is Captain Amstutz's third troller, and all of them have been powered by Caterpillar. He lives in Nanaimo with his wife and two sons ... who will fish with him this summer.

The boat made the cover of that issue.

From their first successful load to the last one, Frank and Blanche were more than happy with how the *Fan Isle* performed. "A little rough weather didn't seem to make much difference," said Frank. "[The Wahl boats] rode awful good in the sea. Some boats you know list over and stay there. The *Fan Isle* would carry 2,600 pounds in the hold. Several times I had it full." Blanche was more reserved in her judgment. "I prayed they were good boats when we were in the middle of a Hecate Strait storm," she said.

"Sometimes it was pretty doubtful."

Fishing was always a family affair in the Amstutz family. Not a season went by that Blanche and their two sons, Joe and Jack, weren't with Frank aboard the *Fan Isle*.

"Before they started school, they were on the boat all the time and after they went to school we went out every summer," Blanche said. "Jack was pulling, I cleaned the fish and Joe did the icing. For fun we put little driftwood boats floating in the ocean that had little stick poles—we got the sticks off the beach—and a paper sail on them. We dropped them going one way to see how many we could see on the way back." (Joe eventually had his own Wahl boat built, the *Loretta A*.)

Despite having great success for four years with the *Fan Isle*, Frank wanted yet a bigger boat and in April 1965 he was on the phone to Wahls for a third time. Henry agreed to the order but explained that construction wouldn't start until the summer so he could keep his crew together. "There was nothing going on that summer," Frank said, "other than some repair work. They built the *Ocean Roamer* as fill-in work, see. Henry told me it was a damn good deal for both of us."

Frank designed the cabin with a galley on deck and a two-bed stateroom. Down below in the fo'c'sle were additional sleeping quarters. For power he threw in, not surprisingly, another Caterpillar. With a length of 56 feet and a beam of 15 feet, the *Ocean Roamer* gave Frank more than ample fish hold capacity, a roomy interior and great stability on the open seas. "That

SEAGOING VOLKSWAGEN

Some folks put their boat on their car to take a trip, but Frank Amstutz do just the reverse. Pictured here is Frank's new fishing vessel, 56' long 15' beam, on its arrival at Richardsons Marina from Prince Rupert B.C. Frank drove north in his Volkswagen to accept delivery, and it was, no problem to take the car aboard for the trip to Nanaimo. Mrs. (Blanche) Amstutz flew to Prince George to make the first trip with Frank.

Nanaimo Times Photo.

The Volkswagen "car"go made headlines in a local Nanaimo paper.
FRANK AND BLANCHE AMSTUTZ COLLECTION

boat could be used for anything—trolling, seining, halibut, anything," he said. "That way it would be easy to sell, see. That's why I had it built so big." Its specifications, which went against the grain of conventional troller design, made the *Ocean Roamer* the largest troller on the BC coast, but marine architects declared it was simply too big to be an effective troller—just as they had said of Leo Carter's *Escapade*. And just as Leo had proved them wrong, Frank would, too.

The *Ocean Roamer* was launched in January 1966, in typical Prince Rupert style—in a downpour. But as the boat hit the water, the sun broke through the clouds, providing a moment that made the event much more memorable. Frank and Blanche had driven up from Nanaimo in their Volkswagen Bug to take delivery of the boat and had no choice but to load the car onto their new boat for the trip back down through the Inside Passage.

Frank had great success with his new Wahl boat, but he didn't enjoy it for long. Unfortunately his health problems flared up again and, as Blanche had to stay home to take care of Joe who was still in school, he found the long periods of separation from his family unbearable. In 1968 Frank quit fishing, a choice he later regretted. "I fished that boat three years and then I quit, but I shouldn't have. I should have stuck it out another few years because that's when the prices were good." But as he had kept the boat well maintained, he didn't lose a penny on the sale.

The *Ocean Roamer* eventually came into the hands of the well-known fisherman Bruce Whittaker, who also owned the Wahl boat *Storm Prince*. The *Fan Isle* is now in the hands of Bruce's good friend Jim Donnelly, who says the boat is in good shape and still has her original Cat engine.

The Company Workboats

The company workboats, vital components in the business, deserve special recognition since they are in the memories of so many people. In the morning the workboat was a ferry, bringing crew members from Prince Rupert to the boatyard at Dodge Cove. During the day it was a supply transport, splitting its time between hauling nails, bolts and paint from town and hauling loads of lumber from either the Wahl mill or John Group's sawmill to the boatyard. A minor role for it was as a runabout for Ed when he had to go to town on business.

The first workboat was *Black Elsie*, a double-ender fishing boat. Classified as a "terrible contraption," it wasn't suitable for transporting heavy freight so didn't last very long. The replacement for it was *WB*, the most famous of the workboats. "It was a big gillnetter," Iver said. "She was 35 feet long and 11 feet in the beam. Melvin Closter was the guy who ran it—well, it was between him and Jack Omori." Malcolm Elder described it as "a general-purpose

Bruce Moore, a machinist by trade, worked for the Wahls for two years in the late 1960s and was given the job of lining up engines in the cannery gillnetters, putting in the controls and doing the shaft work. But he was also responsible for picking up lumber from Oona River. Using the company boat *WB*, he regularly towed a 40-foot by 20-foot scow full of lumber from Oona River to the Prince Rupert Boatyard. "I would leave the Co-op in Rupert at six thirty in the morning," Bruce said, "and come back at seven o'clock at night. I used to go up to the Prince Rupert Boatyard at high tide and then shove the load up onto the ways. In the morning they'd walk down and pick the lumber up."

The Trade Wind, *a 42-foot troller, was built in 1960 for Jack Prince (Sr.), most likely at the Prince Rupert Boatyard.* JACK PRINCE COLLECTION

boat. I don't think it was intended in the first place as a workboat—it just ended up that way. It went on and on for years [as a workboat]. She drew a little less water and they'd go down to the mill and put up a load of lumber and [be back] into town fairly fast."

What the initials "WB" stood for is up for debate. "Work Boat," "Wahl Boat" and "Wahl Brothers" are all reasonable choices but no one, not even my grandfather, knew for sure.

When a second *WB* was built, it was named simply *WB II*. It received the Caterpillar engine from the *Island Queen*.

When things finally slowed down at the boatyards, a company workboat was no longer needed. *WB* went to Iver, who turned it into a fishing boat. "The last time I seen it down south," he said, "a guy was fishing halibut with it." *WB II* went to Paul Armour of the Armour Salvage Company, who used it as a tugboat for his company.

The Prince Rupert Boatyard Fire

In early 1967, after thirty years of operation, the Wahl boat-building business had its first—and only—major disaster when very early one morning fire broke out in the boiler room at the Prince Rupert Boatyard. "I remember it like it was yesterday," Henry's son, Ed, said. "What happened is they had a watchman there and he used to get up early in the morning and put the fire on to get up steam. There was a bunch of shavings right in front of [the boiler] and I guess when the hatch was opened, a spark came out and caught the shavings on fire. About seven o'clock in the morning Irene [the bookkeeper] came down. I was outside having coffee with a corker and she came hollering out of the shop, 'The shop is on

The charred hulk of the original Rennell Sound *sitting on the cradle.*
ROSS HOLKESTAD COLLECTION

fire!' I ran in there and the whole [south] end of the shop was up in flames by that time. I managed to get a couple of boats off the ways [two tugboats that were on the lower sections of the cradle] and then I tried to get this other one off—the *Rennell Sound*. We'd just finished the interior and everything. It was all ready to go and it caught fire."

Rodney Philippson witnessed the fire in its early stage after docking his boat at the Co-op plant. "I'd put my boat on the beach that morning behind the net loft about six o'clock and then I went in the back door of the net loft. I'd seen this smoke, [but] you'd see it every morning coming out the top of the shed when they started the boilers, so I ruled out there was a problem. I came out shortly after and, boy, was the smoke streaming out! Of course, I went in and phoned the fire department—I think mine was the phone call that got them there—and then I waited for the fire department to come down. We hooked up the hydrant and ran hose to the shed and then we hooked up a second hose from the other two-and-a half-inch port. That's all we had to fight with. We had two trucks down there but we just didn't have the pressure. We tried hard. I was in there at the door with water on the side of [the *Rennell Sound*] but we couldn't get around to the other side of the building because there was no door."

The fire consumed approximately half of the south side of the boat shop. The *Western Viking*, which was sitting half planked on the north side of the building floor at the time, received slight fire damage to the top part of its stem. That, in addition to the slightly charred ceiling trusses, was the extent of the damage on the north side. It took about three months to completely rebuild the boat shop but operations resumed in a surprisingly short time.

After the fire, the *Rennell Sound*, a 48-foot combination troller–halibut boat, sat on the cradle in a terrible state. It appeared to have been completely destroyed and the decision was made to scrap it and tow the hulk to a nearby beach. Work on a new *Rennell Sound* began as soon as the boat shop was rebuilt. However, a salvage assessment of the original *Rennell Sound* determined that the boat could be saved since at least one side of the hull was intact. It was dragged off the beach and hauled back into the shed.

Qitonsta *on her launching day.*
RYAN WAHL COLLECTION

Then over the summer a crew led by Iver replaced the burned sections with fresh lumber and completely rebuilt the wheelhouse. The boat was then put up for sale "on spec" and eventually sold.

Young Ed also recalled that, before the fire at the Prince Rupert Boatyard, a much less severe fire-related incident had occurred at the Wahl Boatyard. "A boat called *Lucky Star I* was up on the ways and Uncle Bobby said to the guys, 'Now, don't come close to that thing with a match because there are lots of fumes coming out of it.' Well, one of the guys opened the hatch and flicked a lighter and away she went. Blew the whole top off the boat. The only injury to the guy was singed hair and eyebrows. He was

Sam Maki with Velmar, *Waddington Harbour, BC, 2002.* SAM MAKI COLLECTION

lucky. There was lots of damage and a whole new cabin had to be built. I remember them doing that. Apparently Uncle Roald was working in the shop at the time and a piece of glass went flying right past his ear."

Although the Wahls experienced two tragedies in the 1960s, Ed's death and the disastrous fire, the decade ended well with a spectacular celebration—the launching party for Sam Maki's troller, *Velmar.* This kind of party is the ultimate way to express congratulations to the new owner and his family and wish him luck with a boat that takes

Roald backing Velmar *out of the boatyard.*
MARY WAHL COLLECTION

SEPTEMBER, 1970

WESTERN
FISHERIES

54-Foot Combination Troller-Drum Seiner "Velmar"
Powered With 240 HP Caterpillar Diesel

VELMAR

FINNING
VANCOUVER TO PRINCE RUPERT
CATERPILLAR
CATERPILLAR AND CAT ARE REGISTERED TRADEMARKS OF CATERPILLAR TRACTOR CO., PEORIA, ILLINOIS

marine
MARINE ENGINES • PARTS • SERVICE

with it a bit of the heart and soul from each member of the building crew.

"I've been fishing since … well, I was in Rivers Inlet with my dad," Sam said. "He wasn't a real fisherman—he fished a bit but he was more of a logger. I fished steady since I was thirteen years old. I fished halibut in the Bering Sea. My first boat was nicknamed the *Black Banana* and then the next year I ran the seiner *Anna S*, which was a Skog boat originally from Cassiar. They'd leased it out to Tolluch Western and I went and picked it up. In 1962 I bought the *Telcrest*, a 60-footer built by a Chinese [shipwright] in Victoria in 1926. I'll tell you, what a sea boat! You couldn't make it roll. She was deep like a steamship but had a short keel. And fast! She cruised at ten knots but could do twelve or thirteen with that big engine. Once we made a trip from the fuel dock at Coal Harbour in Vancouver to Sointula in seventeen hours fifty-five minutes. It normally takes twenty-plus hours."

As much as Sam enjoyed the *Telcrest*, after a few years he went on a hunt for a new boat. "First, my brother-in-law, Dickie Michelson, and I went down to Queensborough. He was going to get a steel one built. When Dickie backed down on that, the price would have gone up, so I backed down, too. And then we tried Nanaimo Shipyards but they were going to have plywood decks and I didn't want that. Then one cold bloody winter day I flew up to Rupert by myself—this was nothing to do with my brother-in-law anymore—to meet Bobby. We made a handshake deal and then I paid the bill."

The Wahls showed Sam the 54-foot *Qitonsta*, which they had built in 1968, and Sam went with the same

Opposite: *The* Velmar *on the cover of* Western Fisheries.
COURTESY OF INDUSTRIAL ILLUSTRATORS, *WESTERN FISHERIES* MAGAZINE

Velmar *and the* Island Girl's *were the two biggest boats ever built at* Wahl Boatyard. ART STACE-SMITH COLLECTION

design though he wanted his boat a little higher. Iver built the hull and Roald the wheelhouse, and Sam was amazed at their speed and efficiency. "In six and a half days they planked that sucker. Iver did it, you know, by eye … I don't doubt there were some measurements in the end, but he cut all those damn planks by eye."

For five weeks as the boat was being built, Sam was a guest at Bobby's house. During his stay he became more than a customer to the Wahl family, so after learning that Sam and his family had put every last dollar they had toward the boat, the Wahls were motivated to put on the launching party of all launching parties for him and his new 54-foot by 15-foot combination drum seiner–troller, the *Velmar*. Sam brought in his immediate family from out of town to help celebrate and the party began on June 7, 1969. This being a very special occasion, the boat sliding out of the shed and into the water was just a small portion of the overall celebration. Music and drink were also part of the festivities, with the music being supplied by members of the Wahl family—Roald on the guitar, for one, keeping everyone entertained throughout the night.

When recollecting that day, Sam always has a smile on his face. Receiving the boat from the Wahls was "like sending [me] off with one of their children," he said. "It was a big moment in our lives because we were really poor and we never thought that we would ever have anything like that, you know. So it was a very large moment in our lives. And you know what? I was the first one who ever brought their family for a launching like that. It was a wonderful feeling. They shook my hand and, when we parted, we even cried. But I did see Bob and Roald one more time when Dickie was having the *Island Girl's* built."

Sam's "working boat" has held up well since it was launched almost forty years ago, thanks to his extremely good care of it. "I've never had to replace planks. There was one deck clamp on the port side we had to change and that was all. And a few ribs have gone down below so we put some new ribs in. She's never been recorked and she doesn't leak a drop. It's looked after because we've taken pride in it. A lot of people don't believe that the boat is that old now. Once this gillnetter came to me in Hakai Pass [and said,] 'I see they built another new seiner.' I said, 'Thank you for the compliment. This boat is twenty years old.'" Today the *Velmar* is Sam's yacht and he spends much time aboard. His son owns the *Island Spirit*, built by Ernest Wahl, which has also been converted into a yacht.

Christen (Dickie) Michelson, Sam's brother-in-law and another hard-working Sointula fisherman, liked what he saw in the *Velmar* and so asked the Wahls to build a similar boat for him. It is the 56-foot *Island Girl's*. These two boats were the biggest ever built at the Wahl Boatyard.

CHAPTER EIGHT

THE FAMILY BUSINESS ENDS

I n the early 1970s the Prince Rupert Boatyard was running a twenty- to twenty-five-man crew that, as well as doing routine maintenance and repair, was dealing with extensive reconstruction on aging boats. The most popular operations were still reconfiguring double-ender gillnetters and trollers to give them transom sterns, and building new wheelhouses. New construction in these years was highlighted by the 65-foot packer-seiner *BC Safari*, built for the 1971/72 fishing season, and the 56-foot seiner *Mary Roberta*, built a couple of years later. These were in addition to the half a dozen trollers and gillnetters that were built in the two boatyards. Overall, however, the rate of new construction was down considerably from only a few years earlier.

The times of great change in the fishing industry were no longer on the horizon but on the Wahls' front doorstep. The era of the bulk replenishment of the cannery gillnet boats had ended. The consolidation of canneries and advancements in the canning process meant fewer canneries were required, resulting in many of them shutting down. Thus, when the ten-year cycle for the canneries' wooden gillnetters came to an end in the late 1960s, there were still plenty of the old ones around and little need to build any more.

Speeding the demise of wooden boat building were

the other, "better" materials that were increasingly being used. Since the mid-1960s, fibreglass and aluminum had been gaining in popularity as construction materials, but initially the high manufacturing costs of these materials made them unaffordable to the average boat buyer. It also took a while for the fishermen's skepticism about them and their manufacturing techniques to disappear. Aluminum, in particular, was slow to be accepted, but BC aluminum boat-building leaders and innovators such as Sam Matsumoto, who built whole fleets of aluminum boats in the 1960s, helped increase confidence in this material. Being stronger, lighter in weight and more

One of the 65-foot boats, Western Viking *(now* Endeavour*) or BC* Safari, *under construction at the Prince Rupert Boatyard. These two boats were the largest built by the Wahls out of their North Coast boatyards.* PHOTO COURTESY ROALD AND VIOLET WAHL

durable and (arguably) requiring less maintenance than wood, aluminum gradually became the easy choice for most buyers.

The use of steel had also sent waves of change through the commercial boat-building industry as early as the 1950s. At first fishermen watched closely and scrutinized fishboats built of steel, as they had boats built of fibreglass and aluminum, but acceptance of steel came more swiftly because, especially in Prince Rupert, they had seen it used in the construction of minesweepers and freighters during World War II. The first BC steel seiner was built in 1957. Then, year after year, larger, more powerful and more advanced seiners were launched from BC boatyards, demonstrating that steel was gradually conquering the 50-foot-and-over market.

By the early 1970s the tide had turned noticeably in favour of non-wood materials, resulting in fewer orders for wooden boats of all types. This was a signal to all boatyards to adapt to the new materials or go out of business. The Wahl family talked about getting into aluminum and steel, but with orders for their wooden boats still solid, they saw no reason to do this—yet. They had no choice, however, but to get into fibreglass to some degree as not doing so would have meant turning away too much business. Unfortunately both Henry and Iver suffered while working with fibreglass, which took away any enjoyment in building boats from it. "As a family we would have gotten into fibreglass," Iver said. "We did a few repair jobs and that's how we found out we couldn't work with it."

Norman Iverson was working at the Prince Rupert Boatyard when the Wahls were getting into hand-laying fibreglass. "They were doing some but not a lot. When they built the *BC Safari*, that wheelhouse and dodger and all that stuff was glass and Bobby made arrangements with

The Pagan Isle, *built in 1963 at Prince Rupert Boatyard, in full trolling mode.*
COURTESY OF VANCOUVER MARITIME MUSEUM

some fibreglass outfit in Vancouver to come up and glass that. The guys in the shop were mucking around with it, too, a little bit. It isn't bad if you're all rigged up for it like these guys from Vancouver—like using a chopper gun. When you're hand-laying it up, you know, it's quite different. I'd never heard of a chopper gun when I was over there. I never even knew there was such a thing. I thought it was all done with matting and roving. It's pretty gooey stuff to be playing around with by hand."

Although the Wahls finally did use fibreglass in upper construction, including wheelhouses, neither of their boatyards ever built fibreglass hulls. Instead, after fishermen started approaching them about using the popular pre-made, 36-foot "Pelagic" fibreglass hulls as the basis for turnkey vessels, the Wahls began bringing them in for use in the Prince Rupert Boatyard. The hulls—built on the Lower Mainland—were shipped, one inside another, from Vancouver by barge. After arriving at the Rivtow dock in Prince Rupert, the hulls were dumped off the barge and towed south to the boatyard. The Wahl crew then put up their wheelhouses and installed the decking, engine and all the rigging and gear. The *Little Current*, *Irene C* and *Miss April No. 1* all began as Pelagic hulls that were turned into fully functioning fishing boats.

With this successful leap into modern materials and with the servicing side of the boatyards busier than ever, the family seemed destined for continued success in the foreseeable future. But everything changed with the deaths of Bobby on October 14, 1973, and Henry eleven months later on September 12, 1974, both from complications of diabetes. Bobby was forty-five and Henry fifty-two. "You know, [Bobby] had that diabetes a long time before he ever knew he had it," his wife, Marge, said. "The doctors told him to only work four hours a day but [he worked] more like fourteen. But you can't fault anyone. Everybody has to live their life the way they want. When Grandpa Ed was alive, he expected them to run, not walk, around the job."

Their deaths were the beginning of the end of the business. Shortly before his death, Bobby had taken over management of the Prince Rupert Boatyard from Henry. When Bobby died, the management duties would have gone to Iver as the eldest surviving son, but he opted to stay on the floor. Ernest had already moved south to start his own business, so Roald took over instead. The huge workload didn't worry him and he proceeded to take care of business, though at this point there was essentially only one boatyard to manage because production at the Wahl Boatyard had declined noticeably since the turn of the decade. The family had questioned the feasibility of operating two boatyards even before the deaths of Henry and Bobby, which just sped up what was already inevitable. The remaining Wahl brothers closed the boatyard in Dodge Cove to commercial operations, though it did remain open for the odd commercial job and personal projects.

Roald's tenure as boatyard manager, however, was a short one. In 1975 he and Violet decided to move to Sechelt; it was simply time for them to leave the business and the high demands that went with it. The next question was, which family member would take the reins? Reidar was still working at the Prince Rupert Boatyard at the time but had no interest in managing the operation. Bobby's eldest son, Martin, had taken over as floor foreman there and in this role had proven himself as a capable leader with a potential for management. But any chance of him taking the top job disappeared after he was in a serious car accident and was no longer able to work

Malcolm Elder aboard his former boat, the Chilco.
RYAN WAHL COLLECTION

in the same capacity. "There wasn't anyone [left] to grab the bull by the horns," my uncle Larry said. "[Martin] was the one that was going to do it, I guess. Everybody [else] was kind of done."

Ernest's three sons—Brian, Gordon and Calvin—and Reidar's son Alan talked about taking over but took no action and, with no one in the family willing to take the reins of the business, the decision was made to sell the Prince Rupert Boatyard. The buyer was a family friend; before coming north to purchase the boatyard, Allan Okabe had been working with Ernest on the Lower Mainland. In 1976 Prince Rupert Boatyard became Okabe Shipyards. Allan upgraded some of the facilities and installed a new cradle, and under his ownership it continued to serve the needs of the local fishing fleet into the 1980s.

Even thirty years after the sale of Prince Rupert Boatyard, Malcolm Elder still shakes his head about how things were run there. "It wasn't a building shed," he said. "It was set up more as a repair place. They should have put a long building shed beside it where you start a boat over here and you push it sideways, maybe on rails or rubber tires. You work on four or five boats at a time. See what I mean? You put the ribs up here, you move it over, put the planks on here. You gain quite a bit from that. They had a big lumber shed on the side towards the Co-op plant [that] was on good hard ground. They should have put in a long narrow shed there and moved the boats through on rails. They had room enough for it but I think the capital ran out.

"They didn't need [that] damn big boiler. You either had to keep a fire going all night—which we did some-times when I was there because I lived there—or else if you were going to want to steam in the morning, you had a wait an hour to get steam up. Henry should have bought a steamer that could be flashed up in five minutes—you start it up, wait five minutes, get your steam and then shut 'er down. But he might have to spend a few cents and he might have to do things different than he did yesterday. I argued with Henry about this."

In spite of his admiration for the Wahl family's boat-building capabilities, Malcolm questioned their business sense. "Ol' Ed, he was very honest and a good-hearted man. I've seen him several times do favours for people. The boys, by and large, were the same … They took in an awful lot of [money] but there wasn't too much pausing in their pockets. It was all going out here and there. They were no good at collecting money. They would have done better financially if they'd had a business partner. Get somebody in who knows. They were good but they were backwoods boat builders. If Henry had been more educated, he could have taken a tour down to the American yards and things like that every three, four or five years, and it would have been a lot different picture. I mentioned this to Ernest one time and I said, 'It's so obvious you're losing here and there,' and he said, 'Can you imagine an outsider moving in with this mob?' So they were aware of the need. A partner would have been the best thing if they could have got the right type of man.

"One time Ernest was down to Vancouver and he went to … the chandlers to buy brass fittings. Well, the guy just was so glad to see him because he knew they were building boats. He says, 'If you could send me a $2,000 order or something like that, I'll cut the price in half." They were paying pretty well over-the-counter prices. Well, they couldn't [give him an order of that size] because they were operating a lot of the time just out of the bank. And Fyfe Smith [the lumberyard of J. Fyfe Smith Company Ltd. of Vancouver] was a fair-sized outfit. If they could have given Fyfe an incentive to keep some [hardwoods] on hand—because, you see, they're bidding against other guys down here. I asked Ernest one time, 'Why can't you give him a little more money and get him to lay some aside just for you? They pretty well know what you're ordering.' But [the Wahls] just weren't thinking of paying that extra money."

CHAPTER NINE

THE TRADITION CONTINUES

While Wahl boat-building was ending in the mid-1970s in Prince Rupert, the tradition was well established elsewhere in BC, which was the start of individual boat-building endeavours of Ed' descendants.

In the mid-1960s Ernest Wahl left Prince Rupert and started his own boat-building operation at Salmon Arm, a town of about fifteen thousand people located in south-central British Columbia, midway between Vancouver and Calgary. At about 285 miles from the ocean, the location is an odd one in which to be building commercial fishing boats, but Ernest made it happen. He transformed a 60-foot by 20-foot, two-storey chicken coop on the property into a boat shop and started to build. After each boat was launched out of the shed, it was loaded onto two truck beds—the hull on one and the wheelhouse on the other—and hauled down to the Fraser River where a large crane dropped the engine, the tanks and then the cabin onto the hull. Via interior cabin access panels down by the floor, he attached rods to the cabin and hull to fasten them together. It took a couple of days to complete the connection and then the final step in the process was lifting the finished boat up and setting it into the river. Ernest built a half-dozen boats at this Salmon Arm shop,

The Sandy Point *under construction and leaving the shop for the Fraser River.*
ERNEST AND KAY WAHL COLLECTION

beginning with the *Sandy Point*, followed by the *Janice Ann*, the *Lady Elaine*, the *Spirit of BC* and its sister ship, the *Golden Sands*.

In 1971 Ernest moved his family to Longview, Washington, to undertake the first of two eleven-month-long contracts to build trollers. "He was down there on a work visa," explained Brian, the eldest of Ernest's three sons. "A bunch of fishermen had got together and sort of sponsored him. They'd seen Dad's boats and other Wahl

At 48 feet by 14 feet, the Janice Ann *was the largest boat built in Ernest's Salmon Arm boatyard.* ROALD AND VIOLET WAHL COLLECTION

as Anyone Seen My Boat?

The *Spirit of BC*, the fish packer Ernest Wahl built at his Salmon Arm shop for Dave Carlson in 1968, has sometimes been the focus of attention for the wrong reasons. The first time it made the headlines was in 1993 after the New Democratic Party provincial government tried to register the name of the newest vessel in the BC Ferries fleet as the *Spirit of British Columbia*. Vessel registration is similar to the title systems used for land registry: a name already registered must be preceded or followed by a letter, word or number to distinguish the second vessel from the original. So initially Captain Peter Ady, the superintendent of the Coast Guard, rejected the government's choice of name because in a mayday situation considerable confusion could occur.

At that point, according to a letter to the editor Dave Carlson wrote, which was published in the June 1993 issue of *Western Fisheries*, BC Ferries contacted him with an offer to pay the cost of transferring the name to them, $80. "Very magnanimous of them," Carlson wrote. "I was interested in selling my boat at the time as I had been fired by BC Packers ... The

The Spirit of BC *moments before being dropped into the Fraser River.*
MARY WAHL COLLECTION

The original owner of the Spirit of BC *was first embroiled in a boat name controversy and then had his boat stolen shortly thereafter. Naturally, this left him very dispirited.*

ERNEST AND KAY WAHL COLLECTION

his mind and allowed the new ferry to be called the *Spirit of British Columbia*. And the day after the story appeared in the newspaper, Carlson's boat was stolen from the Annieville Slough where it had been moored. He was told that the *Seaspan Trojan* had spotted his boat off Steveston and that the boat had been tracked by Vancouver Traffic (Vancouver Port Authority) as far as Porlier Pass, but both reports proved to be incorrect. He was absolutely sure that "the only place one could hide [his boat was] in a boat house. Had anyone tried to scuttle her, it is doubtful she would sink because of the wooden hull and the foam-insulated fish holds. "If anyone tried to burn her, the smoke would have attracted someone." He offered a reward of $5,000 for information leading to the recovery of his boat and eventually the *Spirit of BC* was found in Bellingham sporting a new name and carrying a load of high-tech equipment used for smuggling. It was returned to its owner and now, fifteen years later, it still fishes under its original name.

government could have bought my boat and done what they pleased with the boat and name. After spending $137 million on the ferry, a few more thousand wouldn't have been noticed." However, the government didn't offer to buy the boat and Carlson dug in his heels. "As long as I own the boat," he wrote, "the name stays with her!"

Next, according to a front-page story in the *Vancouver Sun* on January 28, 1993, Captain Ady, having received "a high-profile call from the BC Ferry Corporation," changed

The Désirée III, *built in 1973 at the Kent Street shop. "It was the nicest troller on the BC coast," claimed Roald.*
ROALD AND VIOLET WAHL COLLECTION

The Marnie, *built in 1976, inside the Kent Street shop.*
MARY WAHL COLLECTION

boats and that's what they wanted for their trollers down there." But the boats had to be built at the customers' location due to a US federal law called the Jones Act (also known as the Merchant Marine Act) that prohibits foreign-built vessels from being used in a commercial capacity in US waters. This time Ernest converted a cow barn into a boat shop—one step up from a chicken coop. "It wasn't uncommon to go to work and see the cows on one side of you," Brian said. On the first trip he built a 38-foot troller and two that were about 42 feet in length and on the second trip three 48-foot trollers.

The Lorenda Lynn *(now the* Vicious Fisher*).*
ERNEST AND KAY WAHL COLLECTION

The Venturous. MARY WAHL COLLECTION

Long-time Dodge Cove resident John Leakey (right) *helping out with the launching of the* Nordic Rand, *built by Iver at the former Wahl Boatyard.* MARY WAHL COLLECTION

The 76-foot-long Lorenda Lynn *was one of the largest wooden hulls built in western Canada.* MARY WAHL COLLECTION

(Nancy Lath...)

'Ingibjorg K' launching

Several hundred people gathered Saturday afternoon for the launching of the pride of the Dodge Cove Boatyard, the 'Ingibjorg K', which was crafted by master shipwright Ivar Wahl for the owner Brian Kiesman.

A sign hanging on the wall above the assembly summarized the boatyard philosophy: "If God wanted us to have fibreglas boats, He'd have made fibreglas trees."

The 'Ingibjorg K', a 50-foot trawler halibut boat, is crafted from solid mahogany with teak decking and teak interior.

Boatyard owner Alec Spiller says the boat represents the finest effort to date of the Dodge Cove Boatyard. The launching was heralded as the passing of an era because to build such a boat would now cost in excess of a quarter of a million dollars.

The champagne bottle, heavily scored, exploded of its own accord, and the launching was delayed while another was fetched from town.

Pictured above, on the bridge of the boat, are Alex Spiller, Tom Spiller, Ivar Wahl, Mark Stevensen, Steven Ley, Brian Kiesman, Cliff Stegavig, Pat Holt and John Leaky.

The vessel was dedicated to Kiesman's mother who died a few months ago.

Ernest returned to Canada in 1973 and took over a boatyard on Kent Street on the north arm of the Fraser. Here he employed fourteen men including his two eldest sons, Brian and Gordon, and Reidar's son Alan. It was a busy shop as demand was high for repair and new construction of trollers and 50-foot and 60-foot seiners, as well as a few pleasure craft. Wood was the primary construction material but they also did some fibreglass hull finishing.

In the late 1970s Ernest moved his operation to River Road in North Delta where he continued to build both fish and pleasure boats. Those built here included the *Northern Husky* (now *Joy-C-Lynn*), the *Richmond Star*, the *Nordic Gold*, the *Nordic Venture* and the *Larissa*. But it was also from Ernest's North Delta shop that the two largest Wahl boats ever built were launched: the *Lorenda Lynn* and the *Venturous*. The 76-foot, million-dollar *Lorenda Lynn*, built in 1980 for the black cod fishery, was constructed of wood instead of the more popular steel and aluminum because the owner preferred the inherent stability and comfort of wood. It was probably the last wooden hull in western Canada to be built that large. The *Venturous*, built the previous year, is slightly smaller than the *Lorenda Lynn* but still dwarfs most other commercial fishing boats. These two projects came late in Ernest's career. He retired from his North Delta boat shop and from boat building altogether in 1983.

In 1977 entrepreneur Alec Spiller bought the Wahl Boatyard on Dodge Cove. Initially he wanted to keep it running as a repair facility and hired Iver as his master shipwright. Aside from basic repair, including recaulking

Opposite: *An article in the* Prince Rupert Daily News, *May 1980 on the launching of the* Ingibjorg K. COURTESY OF *PRINCE RUPERT DAILY NEWS*

and refastening, Iver and a small crew that included his two sons, Gary and Larry, did a steady stream of conversions, such as replacing outdated sterns with conventional ones. The shop later got into the construction of trollers-longliners, and in a span of two years—1979 and 1980—turned out four 48-foot or 49-foot boats all from the same model. They were the *Miss TJ*, the *Nordic Rand*, the *Ocean Tigress* and the *Ingibjorg K*.

It wasn't long after the launching of the last one, *Ingibjorg K*, that Iver decided to leave the former Wahl Boatyard, but he was kept busy at other local yards doing repairs and renovations. For a couple of years he worked with Norman Iverson at his shed to the north of the former Wahl Boatyard. At Iverson's Iver was commissioned to build a shop workboat and then a work/pleasure boat, the *Northern Spirit*, for Dodge Cove resident Norm Barker. After leaving Iverson's shed, Iver worked at a smaller boat shop on the opposite end of Dodge Cove where he rebuilt a 40-foot pleasure boat, but when he became ill he was forced to quit boat building. He officially retired at the age of seventy-four.

The Third Generation of Wahl Shipwrights

When they were young, most of Ed's grandsons went into the boatyards to work after school and on weekends alongside their fathers and uncles. Henry's son (Ed), Iver's eldest son (my father, Gary), Ernest's three sons (Brian, Gordon and Calvin), Bobby's son (Martin) and Reidar's son (Alan) all eventually made boat building a career.

Iver's younger son, my uncle Larry, worked briefly in the family business before becoming a commercial fisherman. His first job, in the early 1970s, was in the Wahl sawmill where he earned a dollar an hour—the minimum wage at the time was $2.20. The other crew members at the time were Roald and Chris Iverson (Norman Iverson's son). "The reason I went to work in the sawmill was because I quit school," Larry explained. "Well, actually the reason I quit school is I wanted to go fishing so bad. I was fishing with your dad that summer and then I wanted to go fall fishing, but I couldn't go because I had to go to school. So I quit school, but I didn't get to go fishing because Dad told me if I quit school I had to work in the sawmill that winter. In the sawmill we did mainly rough-cut lumber and very little planing. The lumber would be taken out to the drying shed and strip-piled

Gary Wahl's 36-foot gillnetter-troller Huntress *docked at Dodge Cove. It was built in 1973, the year after I was born. He later renamed it* Trina Marie *after my sister. My father was also an accomplished artist, taking special pride in putting the lettering on his boat.* MELAINE FILLION COLLECTION

Gary Wahl with a big catch: a fifty-pound spring salmon.
MARY WAHL COLLECTION

before it was sent to the boatyard. But it wasn't always for
the boatyard. Sometimes we cut orders for other uses and
one in particular I remember was for the old MacMillan
Dock—between the ferry dock and Cow Bay—that used
to be Babcock's."

When Bobby died and Roald took over management of the Prince Rupert Boatyard, Larry moved there
with him and stayed for a couple of winters. As his father
and uncles had done before him, he started out doing
the simple and repetitive tasks such as washing, copper
painting, greasing the cradle and sweeping the floors. He
then got into cementing, recorking, puttying nail holes
and holding onto the end of the planks. "There wasn't much
boat building when I come around there," he observed. "I
remember helping Dad build Martin's boat. We built the
hull over at the Prince Rupert Boatyard and actually I did
quite a bit of work on that boat. There was only Dad and

myself and Gary Morash who helped out with planking. We did quite a few gillnetters, putting on new sterns. A lot of gillnetters and trollers had double-ended sterns and I remember working on a lot of boats to put square sterns on them to make them pack more." Larry currently fishes salmon and cod off his Wahl boat, the *Legacy*.

My father, Gary, specialized in caulking but he was also a commercial fisherman. Iver, my grandfather, explained that Henry had taught my dad everything he knew about gillnetting. "Your dad, he went fishing with [Henry] when he was only that big," Iver explained. "Henry said, 'I'm going to make a fisherman out of that guy,' and your dad really, really liked Henry and wanted to go fishing with him. I said, 'Okay, but you have to look after him.' So that's how your dad started gillnetting. He was really good on that boat, too, and only got better."

When Henry's son, Ed, started out in the Prince Rupert Boatyard he learned much by just observing not only his dad and uncles but others who excelled at their job. "Like the corker Louie Wide. I watched him cork for hours when I was eight or ten years old," Ed said. "I also watched him turn oakum. We called him Popeye because he always had a cigarette in his mouth and it was all crunched up. The arm that he used to hammer was just huge like Popeye's and the other arm was like a toothpick. He was a nice old guy, quite a character."

When Ernest moved to Salmon Arm, he invited Ed to come along with him. There he apprenticed and again learned primarily by example. "Ernie was a good teacher. He didn't really teach you by saying, 'Do this, then this, then this …' But he was methodical in the way he did things and I just kept my eyes open and learned by watching him." Ed remained with Ernest when he moved to the United States to build the trollers, but when

The Ny-Borg *and (*left*) the* Tartu. *The* Ny-Borg *was the first boat in the first batch launched by Sea Master.* RYAN WAHL COLLECTION

he returned nine months later, he took a job with Kris Frostad, a well-known Lower Mainland boat builder. In 1975 the Mutual Marine Insurance Company hired Ed to run its Kanata Marine Ways in Vancouver. This shop was very busy at the time, steadily hauling up yachts as well as commercial boats, though Ed was there for only a year before the shop was forced to close due to high lease prices. But he had little time to wonder what to do next. "What happened was, I worked for Kanata in 1975/76 and then Ralph Meleuchuk called me. He was a commercial fisherman who was really into the fibreglass. He had a troller in his yard that he wanted me to help him with." From that backyard project grew a partnership called Sea Master Boat

Building and Repairs. They worked exclusively in fibreglass and their first order was for a quartet of 42-foot deep-sea trollers, which then became a standard company design. In the span of five years, fifteen or sixteen boats using the same 42-foot by 12-foot-½-inch fibreglass mould were built. Among them were the *Ny-Borg*, the *Born Again*, the *Tartu*, the *Leeb'J* and the *Evening Breeze*. The partnership turned out the odd larger boat as well, including the 52-foot *Ocean Sunset* and the 69-foot *Cape Palmerston*. They also produced

The 52-foot yacht Thunder I, *built by Gordon Wahl in 1984.*
DOUG AND DEB EMERY COLLECTION

The Sea Bear.
ED AND DIANE WAHL COLLECTION

turnkey vessels and made moulds for various boat parts to sell separately. These included hulls, cabins, dodgers, decks, hatch combings, cockpit combings, checkers, cockpit covers and hatch covers.

Despite being a successful venture, the partnership dissolved in 1982 and, after working at a few local boat shops (including managing Trites Marine), as well as for Gordon Wahl for a short time, Ed decided to become an independent shipwright and build yachts. The 65-foot *Sea Bear* was one of them.

For Brian Wahl, Ernest's eldest son, working with his dad and uncles from an early age led to the realization that boat building was what he wanted to do for the rest of his life. "I started at ten years old," Brian said. "Henry paid me twenty-five

The Predator, *built in 1973 by Ernest Wahl.*
ROALD AND VIOLET WAHL COLLECTION

cents an hour. I'd go down every Saturday and every day after school and then I'd come home with Dad. When I was seventeen, I got out of high school and after [working with Dad in] Longview [Washington] went back up to Rupert to work. I stayed there right through that winter till Dad went to Longview the second time. And then I went down there again—I'd had enough of the [Prince Rupert] weather—and since then Dad and I have always been together working."

When Ernest retired, it made sense to Brian and his brothers, Gordon and Calvin, to close the boat shop

The Nordic Star, *built in 1976.*
JACK PRINCE COLLECTION

and move on. They set up elsewhere and worked primarily in fibreglass, but also conducted an experiment with a construction technique called cold-moulding. In this process long, thin, vertical-grain wood veneers are glued together in layers, each layer being laid down in a direction opposite to that of the previous layer. Several layers form a light but rigid hull capable of very high speeds. "It was for a friend of mine," Brian explained. "It was interesting because of the design work that went into it, and it was all fairly new to the market so we were dealing with the manufacturers in the States. They ran my design through their computers and told me how to improve the strength of the structure. It's not like a regular boat inside, with ribs and stuff like that. It's designed so that everything in the interior of the boat contributes to the strength of the hull. This gets rid of weight somewhere else. It's quite an elaborate set-up. There was still a lot a framework in it, but, say, if we were putting a floor in, that floor was designed into the strength of the hull. So instead of putting up timber or extra frames in the hull to make the hull strong in that area, we would put in a floor that's designed to take that kind of pressure. Then we could get rid of that timber and that weight. Everything that went into that boat was designed around that idea—even the cabinetry."

According to Brian, this experimental boat could attain a speed of thirty-eight knots and, if it had become viable as a commercial fishing boat application, it would have been leading-edge in the industry. But construction in this technique didn't go further due to the high cost. "It's a lengthy process and too expensive for a fisherman to buy it. They wouldn't spend that kind of money."

Ernest's sons also got into finishing off the interiors of the popular Deltaga fibreglass hulls and later, after leasing the moulds, building them as well. They also built 22-foot aluminum crew boats. Overall, Ernest's three sons became very adept builders in both wood and non-wood materials.

At the age of twenty-three, Bobby's son Martin started to work at the Prince Rupert Boatyard full-time, eventually becoming the floor foreman responsible for handling the cradle for the larger boats. "I was the floor boss for a while—like assistant manager on the floor," Martin said. "I was handling the carriage and doing all the heavy lifting, you know, hauling the *[Silver] Bounty* and the other heavy boats up. Whenever they had big boats to haul up on that carriage, they'd call me. I pulled up the airport ferry a couple of times." Martin was also responsible for the hiring and firing of the crew, although he didn't have to do much of the latter. "I watched and analyzed how they worked and what they'd do—that's each guy, each greenhorn. I'd give them a job to do and see how long it took and if they did it [right]. The other guys knew what they had to do. We would talk about things on the weekend so they knew what had to be done to this boat and that boat and they were anxious to do it because it gave them a job—these were guys that wanted to work and they liked the boat building. Better than standing there and stacking boxes, you know?"

CHAPTER TEN

TIMES OF CHANGE

T he former Prince Rupert Boatyard didn't operate past the mid-1980s. It was eventually demolished and today there are virtually no remnants of it, no scraps of lumber or even pilings that would serve as reminders of a business that was once so vital to the local fishing industry. Anything lying loose on the beach has had a long time to wash away.

The Wahl Boatyard in Dodge Cove still stands, but it is a mere shadow of what it once was. It now operates as a repair and service facility only. No more commercial fishing boats will be built there.

The Wahl sawmill was sold to my other grandfather, Lawrence Fillion, in the early 1970s. He eventually left it and while dormant it served as a playground for the next generation of the family. Boomed logs became balance beams, abandoned crew bunkhouses became playhouses, huge sawdust piles became hills to conquer. Then Mother Nature slowly reclaimed the site. The salmonberry bushes that proliferate on the island have sprouted underneath the debris of the collapsed sawmill. They are overshadowed by the mighty alders that are replacing those cleared from the site in the last years of the mill's operation.

Dodge Cove itself has changed dramatically over the years. When Ed Wahl and his family arrived, fishing was the common bond that connected the people of the

Mary ("Nan") Wahl and I at Dodge Cove in the summer of 2003.
RYAN WAHL COLLECTION

settlement, but as fishing declined, families either moved away or turned to other industries to support themselves. Today the small complement of fishermen who still live there have been joined by those who simply want separation from the city, and the many artists among them no doubt use the nature-filled environment as their muse. But even today when its residents are much more diversified, Dodge Cove still attracts primarily those who want to be part of a tight-knit community.

The amenities have improved considerably since my great-grandfather's day. Hydro was provided in the early 1960s when the airport was constructed on the northern half of the island; telephone service was brought in shortly after. Most of the residents tie up their boats at the government wharf, although some have their own docks.

Running from one end of the village to the other is the same single road free of traffic lights and transportation is mainly by foot or bike, although ATVs are becoming more and more popular as multi-purpose vehicles. The most common means of transporting goods, though, is still the wheelbarrow, a simple yet effective device whose design principles haven't changed since it was invented by the ancient Greeks centuries ago.

On a visit in 2003, the change I noticed most was the silence. When I was growing up there, you could always hear the sound of kids playing. Now an eerie calm pervades the once hectic community. The innocence and the single road seem to be the only constants in Dodge Cove as the eras pass.

For most of the last century fishing was the backbone of the local and provincial economy. Now all the coastal fishing communities have either died out or undergone major transformations to stay alive, forced to remodel their waterfronts for tourism, which today is one of the biggest sources of revenue for British Columbia. To see how times have changed, you just have to walk down to any marina. Gone are the packs of commercial fishboats so tightly docked together that you could walk from one to the other to get to the next pier. Today it's the sport fishermen's boats that occupy those spaces, which isn't surprising since the tourism and sport fishing industries are so tightly integrated.

"If God had wanted fibreglass boats, he would have made fibreglass trees!" is a saying that can still be seen on wooden boats and the walls of wooden boat shops around the world. But that wood is no longer viable in today's boat-building industry, at least for commercial-sized fish-boats. The stock of edge-grain lumber suitable for boat building has been so depleted that the construction of a wooden boat today is a very costly endeavour. Even if you happen to find enough lumber for a backyard project, regardless of the price paid for the material, the high cost of maintaining a wooden boat today prohibits such projects from even being started. Basically, what has transpired over the last half century of commercial boat building is another battle of tradition versus technology and wood has lost. I imagine this is an outcome that industry analysts could have predicted after iron and steel began replacing wood in shipbuilding midway through the last century.

The last of the large wooden boats were built in the early 1990s and they now represent the last of their kind on the BC coast. In other major marine centres around the world, including Norway, the building of large wooden

The Martina Doria *(formerly the* Free to Wander*), built by Ernest in 1975. "I picked a Wahl boat [for a conversion]," said owner Bill Sherman, "because Wahl is a good name and [their boats] all look good so they are the ideal candidates."* RYAN WAHL COLLECTION

boats has declined so sharply that it is virtually non-existent. Today the strongest support for the continued use of large wooden boats comes in the form of yacht conversions of ex-fishboats. The *San Mateo* is one example; two others are the *Tonga* and the *Martina Doria*.

Wooden fishboats and pleasure boats still exist, however, and need to be maintained, which is why the few traditional shipwrights still around are in high demand. Ed and

The 41-foot Tonga, *built at the Wahl Boatyard in 1965, before (above) and after (below) its conversion.* PAT KUKURUZ COLLECTION

Brian Wahl continue to work as shipwrights, performing repairs and rebuilds. No doubt they will have enough work to keep them busy until they choose to retire, given the number of wooden boats still afloat. But with traditional boat building being a dying industry, they won't be inclined to pass their skills on to their children and this doesn't bode well for the maintenance of large wooden boats in the future.

Fortunately, the passion for wood continues in the construction of smaller craft—rowboats and sailboats. Every year a steady flow of students arrive at Canada's only wooden boat-building school, Silva Bay Shipyard School, and classic boat festivals on the Lower Mainland and Vancouver Island consistently draw large crowds. One even includes a family-oriented small wooden boat-building contest. All these events help to keep the art of wooden boat building alive and, I hope, will continue to do so for many years to come.

EPILOGUE

THE BUILDING OF
THE LEGACY

T he last Wahl wooden fishboat slid off the main building floor at the former Wahl Boatyard in 1990, a full sixty years after Ed built the first one in the same spot. It seemed fitting that this boat went to a member of the family.

Iver, with Larry standing by, outlining the shape of a mould. The scene as described by Malcolm Elder: "Iver is drawing it out on quarter-inch plywood. Each mould is slightly different and he knows in his head what he needs. He's made the model first and then he takes [the shape] off that and puts it on the plywood. When you haven't got the mathematical training, see, you have to do it in these old steps." MARY WAHL COLLECTION

Iver cutting out a plank on the band saw.
MARY WAHL COLLECTION

Larry Wahl began his fishing career on the 36-foot, Vestad-built *Crystal Dawn* as a gillnet fisherman and then, after getting the trolling bug, became a combination fisherman. Eventually he threw out the drum on his boat and just trolled, focussing on the spring salmon of the Queen Charlotte Islands. In 1987, after spending fourteen years on the *Crystal Dawn* and travelling thousands of nautical miles, Larry decided that it was time to upgrade. He set out to find a bigger boat in good shape, preferably one

Martin attaching one end of a plank.
MARY WAHL COLLECTION

Gary using a power sander to sand down the hull. In the old days sanding was all by hand. MARY WAHL COLLECTION

built by the family. He found at least one that seemed like a suitable match but ultimately wasn't satisfied with any of the boats he looked at. "I decided I wanted a little bigger boat. I looked around and really didn't find what I was looking for and then Dad asked if we should build a boat," Larry said.

Iver got busy crafting the half-model that would be the basis for a 38-foot boat. Then, after further thought about what he wanted, Larry had him build a new model for a boat 2 feet longer. "It started off small and then kind of grew a bit," Larry said. "At first we were going to build it to the length of my old boat, but then we decided that was kind of defeating the purpose. We decided on 40 feet to keep it under the steamboat classification."

An important early step was to line up suppliers for all the lumber that would be needed. Ernest, who was retired and living in Surrey by this time, was engaged to help with that task and he tracked down the oak, gumwood and raised plywood needed for the wheelhouse. Then, by good fortune, a large supply of cedar became available at John Group's former sawmill, then run by the Bergman brothers. "I think somebody out there was going to build a boat or something because they had all the planking cut already," Larry said. "But they decided not to build it, so we got all of that planking and some of the yellow cedar."

Production of the 40-foot by 13-foot boat began in December 1989 at the former Wahl Boatyard, now owned by Dave Prosser, who was kind enough to lend his

Iver caulking (or corking) the seams by hammering in strands of dry cotton with a mallet. The cotton swells when it's exposed to water and by doing so, seals the seams to make the boat watertight. This action also makes the hull more rigid because it forces the planks against each other.
MARY WAHL COLLECTION

Right: *The author inside the fish hold. I came up after final exams at college to help out. I fished on* Legacy's *maiden season and for the next few seasons after that.*
MARY WAHL COLLECTION

Below: *Larry puttying the seams. The putty seals in the caulking.*
MARY WAHL COLLECTION

facility. He gave the Wahls their choice of building locations within the shop, but the most logical place was the sloping main floor where in the past the larger boats had been constructed. (First, however, Larry had to improve the floor and the rest of the infrastructure.) Larry was proud to be building his new boat in the same spot his predecessors had built so many hundreds of boats. "It was exciting to build the boat in the old family way," he said, "especially with my dad." Help also came from his brother Gary, and Bobby's son Martin.

On April 26, 1990, long before the sun had risen, the nameless hull was launched into the icy cold North Coast water. When it came time to name it, many ideas were thrown around, but it was the suggestion of Larry's long-time friend and current deckhand David Anderson that hit the nail on the head: the *Legacy*.

Luckily many photos of the construction were taken. The ones presented here were selected to capture the essence of the process from start to finish.

The basic boat-building process step by step

Where it all begins: the boat's backbone. Backbone members from bow to stern: stempost, keel, keelson, shaftlog and sternpost. Stacked to the side on the right are the moulds that will soon attach to it.

MARY WAHL, LARRY WAHL AND TRINA WHITTAKER COLLECTIONS

The moulds have been attached to the keel and the builders are starting to put on the battens, the pieces of wood running the full length of the boat that hold the moulds in place.

MARY WAHL,
LARRY WAHL AND
TRINA WHITTAKER
COLLECTIONS

An inside hull view showing the moulds and ribs (the framing). After being steamed, the ribs are pressed against the battens from the inside to further define the hull shape. At this point in the process the moulds can be removed.

MARY WAHL, LARRY WAHL AND TRINA WHITTAKER COLLECTIONS

Above: *The hull after the moulds have been removed. The battens will be removed as the planking is installed.*
MARY WAHL, LARRY WAHL AND TRINA WHITTAKER COLLECTIONS

Left: *The stern construction is well underway.*
MARY WAHL, LARRY WAHL AND TRINA WHITTAKER COLLECTIONS

The planking is complete and caulking is partially complete.
MARY WAHL, LARRY WAHL AND TRINA WHITTAKER COLLECTIONS

Left: *The completed hull ready to launch.*
MARY WAHL, LARRY WAHL AND TRINA WHITTAKER COLLECTIONS

Below: *After the launch the hull is brought back into the boat shop for the upper construction, including installation of the decking.*
MARY WAHL, LARRY WAHL AND TRINA WHITTAKER COLLECTIONS

The construction of the cabin is underway.
MARY WAHL, LARRY WAHL AND TRINA WHITTAKER COLLECTIONS

The final product resting on the cradle while Larry applies another coat of paint. MARY WAHL, LARRY WAHL AND TRINA WHITTAKER COLLECTIONS

Larry and I heading out to the fishing grounds. The construction of the Legacy *marks the end of an era in British Columbia's history, throughout which master craftsmen like the Wahls kept the fishing industry afloat.*

DAVE PROSSER COLLECTION

Acknowledgements

I would like to recognize and thank those who graciously shared their knowledge, stories, photos and documents. The book wouldn't be the same without their contributions. In alphabetical order, they are:

Frank and Blanche Amstutz
Melvin Closter
Jim Donnelly
Randy Dudoward
Dan Edwards
Odd Eidsvik
Malcolm Elder
Currie Ellis
Agot Erickson
Jan Grude
Heather Kerr
Melaine Fillion (my mother)
Lenny Hadland
Ross Holkestad
Foster Husoy
Helen Iverson
Norman Iverson
Harold and Hilda Johnson
Pat Kukuruz
Jim Moncur
Bruce Moore
Jack Prince

Ken Olsen
Rodney Philippson
Sam Maki
David Rahn
Anton Ramfjord Jr.
Vidar Sandhals
Art Stace-Smith
Norm and Rita Trites
Brian Wahl
Ed Wahl
Ernest and Kay Wahl
Gordon Wahl
Iver and Mary Wahl
Larry Wahl
Martin Wahl
Roald and Violet Wahl
Allana Wallin
Trina Whittaker (my sister, who has the uncanny ability to remember the finest details of growing up on Dodge Cove)

Special thanks goes to the following people who were especially helpful with the project: Kathleen Larkin at the Prince Rupert Library, Melvin Closter's daughter and former Dodge Cove resident Diane Wheeler, Kenneth Campbell, Carl Olafson, and Rob Morris of *Western Fisheries*.

Bibliography

Books

Bennett, Norma V. *Pioneer Legacy: Chronicles of the Lower Skeena, Volume I.* Terrace, BC: Dr. R.E.M. Lee Hospital Foundation, 1997.

Blyth, Gladys. *History of Port Edward, 1907–1970.* Self-published. No date.

Bowman, Phylis. *Muskeg, Rocks and Rain!* Port Edward, BC: Raindrop Books, 1973.

———. *Land of Liquid Sunshine.* Prince Rupert, BC: 1982.

Forester, Joe, and Anne Forester. *British Columbia's Commercial Fishing History.* Saanichton, BC: Hancock House, 1975.

Harris, E.A. *Spokeshute: Skeena River Memory.* Victoria, BC: Orca Book Publishers, 1990.

Large, R.G. *Prince Rupert: A Gateway to Alaska and the Pacific.* 2nd revised edition. Vancouver, BC: Mitchell Press Limited, 1973.

McLaren, T.A., and Vicki Jensen. *Ships of Steel: A British Columbia Shipbuilder's Story.* Madeira Park, BC: Harbour Publishing, 2000.

Skogan, Joan. *Skeena: A River Remembered.* Distributed in Canada by Raincoast Book Distribution Ltd., 1983.

Walbran, Captain John T. *British Columbia Coast Names 1592–1906: Their Origin and History.* Vancouver: J.J. Douglas Ltd., 1971, Douglas & McIntyre, 1991.

Wicks, Walter. *Memories of the Skeena.* Saanichton, BC: Hancock House, 1976.

Newspaper Articles

Along the Waterfront: "Triple Launching culminates lengthy Wahl boatyard building program." *Daily News* [Prince Rupert, BC], 31 Dec. 1959.

Bowman, Phylis. "Free time in a small town." *Daily News EXTRA* [Prince Rupert, BC], 6 Aug. 2004: 2.

Brinton, Stewart. "Have you ever built a boat, Billy?" *Daily News* [Prince Rupert, BC], 1983.

"Ernie Wahl's Vancouver Boatyard." *Daily News Fishing Edition* [Prince Rupert, BC], 1974.

"Hospital saw more picnickers than patients." *Daily News* [Prince Rupert, BC], 7 Apr. 1993: 12.

Pederson, Nadine. "Wahl Enjoyed Family Business." *Daily News* [Prince Rupert, BC], 20 Nov. 1998.

Venis, Rodney. "Dodging the Past." *Daily News* [Prince Rupert, BC], no date.

Waterfront Whiffs: "New Fishing Boats Listed." *Daily News* [Prince Rupert, BC], 30 Mar. 1946.

Waterfront Whiffs: "Wahl Boat Yard at Dodge Cove—Busy Establishment." *Daily News* [Prince Rupert, BC], 2 Mar. 1946.

Magazine Articles

Brinton, Stewart. "The Wahls: A Boat Building Dynasty." *The Westcoast Fisherman,* Aug. 1988: 27–30.

Davey, G.A. "This Month in Prince Rupert." *Western Fisheries,* May, 1955–Mar. 1965.

"Design, Hull Shape, Seaworthiness, Speed and Replacement of Modern Fishing Boats." *Western Fisheries,* Nov. 1951: 15–16.

"Dodge Cove, Digby Island." *Western Fisheries,* Aug. 1946, June 1948, June 1952, Apr. 1954: 44.

Floyd, Dick. "The Wahls Put Wood on the Waves." *The Magazine,* 14 Oct. 1984: 5.

Rahn, David. "Wahl Brothers Start a New Deltaga 41." *The Westcoast Fisherman,* June 1990: 57, 59.

Rysstad, Jean. "A Wahl Boat." *The Westcoast Fisherman,* June 1990: 20–25.

———. "McLean Shipyard." *The Westcoast Fisherman,* May 1990.

"The Story Behind a Boat Launching." *Western Fisheries,* Oct. 1944: 18.

"Waterfront Briefs/The Fishing Fleet." *Western Fisheries,* Mar. 1940–June 1954.

"Why Lumber Is Scarce." *Western Fisheries,* June 1944: 18.

Interviews

Wahl, Iver. Personal interview for an oral history initiative, date unknown.

Tasaka, Jack. Personal interview for oral history initiative.

North Pacific Papers, North Pacific Cannery NHS, Port Edward, BC, date unknown.

Internet Sites

Butler, Caroline and Ken Campbell. "The River People: Living and Working in Oona River." *Forests and Oceans for the Future.* Vancouver, BC: University of British Columbia, 2003. 11 May 2004. <http://www.ecoknow.ca/documents/OonaBook.pdf>.

"Canada—The Great Depression." *Encyclopaedia Britannica.* 2 Apr. 2004. <http://www.britannica.com/EBchecked/topic/91513/Canada>

"Canfisco's Early Years." *West Coast Salmon History*. GoldSeal. 12 Feb. 2004. <http://www.goldseal.ca/wildsalmon/salmon_history.asp?article=8>.

"Emigrants from Trondheim 1867–1930." *Digitalarkivet (Digital Archives)*. National Archives of Norway. 2 Oct. 2006. <http://digitalarkivet.uib.no/cgi-win/webcens.exe?slag=visbase&filnamn=EMITROND&gardpostnr=167259&sokefelt=skjul>.

"History of Prince Rupert Airport." *Prince Rupert Airport*. Prince Rupert Airport Authority. 4 May 2004. <http://www.ypr.ca/html/history.html>.

"Longship." *Wikipedia*. 11 Oct. 2004. <http://en.wikipedia.org/wiki/Longship>.

Menzies, Charles R., "Us and Them: The Prince Rupert Fishermen's Co-op and Organized Labour, 1931–1989." *Labour/Le Travail*.48 (2001): 61 pars. 25 Feb. 2006. <http://www.historycooperative.org/journals/llt/48/04menzie.html>.

Morse, Stephen P. *Ellis Island White Farm (1892-1924*. Oct. 2006. < http://www.jewishgen.org/databases/EIDB/ellis.html.

"Norway and conditions in Norway prior [to] and during the emigration period." *Digitalarkivet (Digital Archives)*. National Archives of Norway. 25 Sept. 2006. <http://digitalarkivet.uib.no/utstilling/eng/norge.htm>.

"Norwegian 1900 census for 1751 Nærø." *Digitalarkivet (Digital Archives)*. National Archives of Norway. 2 Oct. 2006. <http://digitalarkivet.uib.no/cgi-win/webcens.exe?slag=visbase&sidenr=9&filnamn=f01751&gardpostnr=128&personpostnr=957#nedre>.

Petzelt, Barbara. "Preliminary Review of Archaeological Sites in the Fairview Terminal Area, West Side of Kaien Island, Prince Rupert Harbour, British Columbia." Oct. 2004. Prince Rupert Port Authority. 7 Sept. 2005. <http://www.rupertport.com/pdf/envass/Archeology.pdf>.

"Viking." *Wikipedia*. 11 Oct. 2004. <http://en.wikipedia.org/wiki/Viking>.

Weitemier, Kevin A. "Leif Erikson." *Great Norwegians*. Metropolitan News Company. 21 Jan. 2004. <http://www.mnc.net/norway/LeifErikson.htm>.

216

Index